SUTHERLAND'S WAR

G000229156

SUTHERLAND'S WAR

*An English Gentleman
goes into Battle*

DOUGLAS SUTHERLAND

Leo Cooper
in association with
Secker & Warburg

First published in Great Britain in 1984 by
Leo Cooper in association with
Martin Secker & Warburg Limited,
54 Poland Street, London W1V 3DF

ISBN: 0-436-50601-7

Photoset by Rowland Phototypesetting Ltd,
Bury St Edmunds, Suffolk
Printed and bound in Great Britain by
Richard Clay (The Chaucer Press) Ltd,
Bungay, Suffolk

DEDICATION

'You did not really *kill* people in the last war, did you, Daddy?' asked my youngest daughter.

'No, darling,' I replied, after a long pause. 'That was someone else.'

This book is dedicated to all children of all fathers, who long ago were someone else—and particularly to Simon, son of my old friend Colonel Ralph Brassey, because he asked.

CHAPTER 1

The day I joined the Army was like the beginning of a bad French film: rain sleeting down out of a grey sky, indistinct muffled figures hurrying on their way, silhouetted briefly against the dimly-lit windows of a mean café, and in a doorway our hero, dejected-looking, hugging himself to keep warm and trying to summon up enough courage to end it all by plunging into the icy waters of the Seine.

Although I have described the scene accurately enough, the setting was not, in fact, a back-street in Paris but Castle Hill in Edinburgh, and if I, shivering in my doorway, was not exactly contemplating throwing myself off the ramparts of Edinburgh Castle, at least my situation was acutely depressing.

The events leading up to this desperate state of affairs are quickly told.

By reason of an ability to pass examinations with disconcerting ease, I had managed in the previous year to escape at a precociously early age from a grimly monastic boarding school in the Scottish Highlands on the grounds that there were no further academic hurdles for me to leap. My father, who was convinced that anyone who finished up at the end of term anywhere above halfway in the class list was bound to come to a sticky end, was dreadfully alarmed. Obviously something had to be done. Thrashing around for a solution, he suddenly remembered that he had once met a man on a train who had told him that there was a dearth of bright young chaps 'in business'.

This piece of information left such a deep impression on my father that a letter was accordingly written to London and a reply was received from an obviously bewildered Lord Leverhulme, thanking my father for offering him such a golden opportunity and informing him that the Staff Controller of Unilever Limited would be pleased to consider an application 'through the usual channels'.

The result of my father's efforts was that, three months before my seventeenth birthday, I found myself each morning operating one of four elevators, delivering everyone, from the grandest directors of that vast organization down to the humblest office boy, to the various floors on which they worked, and for the rest of my eight-hour day carrying assorted visitors up and down.

It was heady work. My elevator was not a modern push-button air-conditioned capsule. To start it you had to ease a lever forward for smooth take-off and gently press backwards to bring the lift to a halt precisely in line with the floor above. From the moment I passed through the imposing doorway of Unilever House, flanked by great bronze lions and overlooking the Thames, I earned every penny of the 32s. 6d. a week they paid me.

The job had its compensations. I looked resplendent in my smart uniform and peaked cap and, if I conceived a dislike for one of the passengers, I could give him a really bumpy ride and hope he tripped on the step on the way out.

In the meantime my father had informed all and sundry that I was Lord Leverhulme's personal assistant and would shortly step into his shoes. To give him his due, he really believed it.

Alas, my delightful occupation was short-lived. After only a month I was stripped of my livery and 'promoted' to tea-boy in

a department concerned with African trade. Nobody ever explained to me the exact function of this department, but apparently it had something to do with the buying of beads and such trifles to trade with natives in return for a mysterious product which was ultimately turned into margarine.

Soon, however, I was relieved of my tea-making duties and given the once-in-a-lifetime opportunity of becoming a commercial traveller in toothpaste. From that moment my decline was rapid and I started to seek refuge in drink, a state of affairs culminating in that sordid night in Edinburgh.

I had spent the day humping my little bag of toiletries from chemist to chemist. The rain had never stopped. Nobody wanted my bloody toothpaste. Finally, after I had mislaid my bag of samples, I decided to get drunk in earnest. By closing time I had precisely two pennies to my name and the location of my commercial hotel had vanished from my mind. So I went down to Waverley Station, put half my working capital in the slot and settled down as best I could for the night.

The following morning I found myself watching a watery sun struggling to rise above the ramparts of Edinburgh Castle, while I turned my single remaining penny over and over in my pocket in an effort to derive some small comfort from its possession. Nearby a clock struck nine and, as the last note sounded, on the opposite side of the street a shop window was suddenly illuminated. There was the sound of bolts being drawn; the door was flung open and, for a moment, silhouetted against the bright light, appeared the magnificent figure of an Army staff sergeant, tartan-trousered, buttons gleaming and a scarlet sash set slantwise across his bemedalled chest. Above the premises I discerned the fateful legend: Army Recruiting Office.

Suddenly the memories flooded back. The elevator operator's uniform—the peaked cap—the authority—the happiness.

I crossed the road.

It was 0915 hours, on the 18th of January; the year was 1939.

The interview which followed was brief. Name? Age? Occupation? To which last enquiry the staff sergeant wrote down 'None' without waiting for the formality of a reply.

'Right. Down corridor, second left. Clothes off. Await medical officer's inspection.'

It was an order. I did as I was told. It is a habit you learn fast in the Army.

I had not long to shiver before the MO appeared. 'Sutherland?' he enquired, eyeing me not unkindly over half-lens glasses. I agreed.

'Read that from top left.' He pointed to a card of letters of the alphabet in decreasing sizes. I complied, adding for good measure 'Printed by Gale and Polden, Aldershot,' which was set in miniscule type at the bottom right-hand corner.

'Ah. Bit of a humorist, are we?' he said drily. 'Right. Tell me when you can't hear this watch ticking.' He held a large half-hunter close to my right ear and then backed away. I kept nodding until he hit the wall. The same thing happened with my left ear.

He then tested my reflexes, told me to stand up and cough a few times while he stared with seeming fascination at my testicles, wrapped up his bag of tricks, wrote something on a piece of paper and prepared to leave.

'Give that to the staff sergeant,' he said, nodding briefly. At the door he turned. 'Good luck,' he said. He was really quite a good sort.

Exactly a quarter of an hour later I was back on Castle Hill fully dressed. But now the proud, if slightly bemused, possessor of a third-class railway warrant for Berwick-upon-Tweed, a working capital of one pound and one shilling, and a card which certified that I was 145084 Private Sutherland D.C.H. of the King's Own Scottish Borderers.

It was 1022 hours on the 18th of January; the year was still 1939.

CHAPTER 2

For quite a while the days were confused.

'Left! Left!

Left! Right! Left!

I had a good home and I Left!

Left! Left!

Left! Right! Left!

A-bout turn!

One two three four!

Halt!

Number two in the back rank, next time you get out of step, I'll kick your arse so hard a shower of pigeons will fly out.'

Number two in the back rank was usually me.

Our lives were regulated by the bugle. Reveille shattered our slumbers at 6 am, followed almost instantaneously by the Company Sergeant throwing open the door of the barrack room with the traditional bellow: 'Come on, let's be having yer. Hands off cocks, feet in socks.'

As 'Come to the Cookhouse Door' was sounded on the bugle, we'd all set off at a dash, mess tins, knife, fork and spoon at the ready, to be first in the queue for porridge and a pint of black tea. We spent the day flogging up and down the barrack square. Whenever there was a break we'd be set to polishing something, from the toe caps and studs of our ammunition boots to the

13

barrack-room floor, and especially the barrack-room floor—
about four times a day.

Initially one of my great trials was mastering the art of
putting on puttees—not simple ankle puttees but yards of serge
to be wrapped tightly and symmetrically to just below the knee.
This masterpiece of sartorial military elegance had to culmin-
ate in exactly the right position, with the fastening on the
outermost side. A fraction of an inch out and it all had to be
done again. Worse, any slackness would result in the whole
thing unwinding, usually on parade, so that it trailed behind
like a roll of lavatory paper thrown at a football match.

'What's the point?' I asked Jacky, an old stager with some
twenty years' service and more, one day.

'Snakes,' he said. 'You don't want to get bitten by snakes, do
you?'

His explanation seemed just as acceptable as any other.

The NAAFI was, and still is, a remarkable organization.
There a young soldier could buy, at incredibly cheap prices,
almost anything his heart desired—cups of tea, rock buns, boot
polish, soap, Brasso—even the very brand of toothpaste I had
so recently been attempting to sell. For the princely sum of 5d I
invested in a pad of writing paper, the sort with lines, a pen with
a nib and a bottle of ink.

Returning to my barrack room I sat on the end of my bed and
wrote two letters. The first was to my late employers, Messrs
Unilever, in which I tendered my resignation and to which I
added, with a fine flourish, that I felt my country needed me
more than they did. The second letter, to my father, was more
difficult to write. Having himself served with distinction in a
Scottish regiment, I played upon his sympathy for my patriot-
ism.

The reply from Unilever was prompt and said that they had
already decided to dispense with my services and would I
kindly return their toothpaste samples. The problem with my

father was resolved when, some time later, I received a letter to the effect that he had been committed to a mental institution.

Thus divested of any form of guilt, I embarked on my military career with dedicated enthusiasm. In fact, so pre-occupied was I with becoming a soldier that the indication that spring was around the corner only came upon me when some-one observed that the tap in the wash house next to our barrack room had become unfrozen.

That was the good news. The bad news was that I'd got myself picked for the regimental boxing team. Lest anyone should think this was a high honour, let me at once disabuse them. It may have been a different matter in the days of the British Raj, when the honour of the regiment was all-important and 'to love the game beyond the prize' was axiomatic. How-ever, with a cadre of raw squaddies all striving for their very survival, this appointment could by no stretch of the imagina-tion be regarded as the cherry on top of the cake.

Being a member of the team entailed reporting to the gymna-sium precisely five minutes after reveille had sounded, dressed in a flimsy white vest and abbreviated blue pants which, on a chorus girl, would have driven every sugar-daddy for miles around mad with desire. What rather spoiled the effect were the thick woollen socks, ammunition boots and boxing gloves.

Weather conditions were considered of no importance. Come blizzard, storm or flood, off we went, grunting and panting over the headlands. Sprayed by the frigid waters of the North Sea, we jogged, trotted and sprinted until we sweated like bulls. Then back in the gym we sparred, did press-ups (anyone unable to do fifty was a cissy), punched unyieldingly heavy sacks, which we were assured were full of dead sergeant-majors, climbed ropes, vaulted bucks and chucked medicine balls around. A badly caught medicine ball hurled unexpectedly by the PT instructor lowered one's chances of producing a family dramatically.

Of course, we had privileges. We ate steak instead of bacon for breakfast and were excused route marches. Instead, we ran up and down mountains.

I looked forward to our first representative match with mixed feelings, terror being the uppermost sensation, followed a close second by the unworthy thought that if I let the side down with sufficient distinction I would be dropped from the team forever and condemned instead to some lesser penance like peeling ton after ton of spuds or cutting the Officers' Mess lawn with nail scissors. Both seemed infinitely preferable prospects.

We were a motley crew. Little 'Dinger' Bell, our flyweight hope, stood around five feet nothing on tiptoe and, having been reared in the Glasgow Gorbals, would fight anything that moved. There were a couple of middleweights—MacConnachie, a red-headed ex-bookmaker's 'minder', and Fergus Campbell, a black-browed Highlander who had been in a spot of bother for pitching a water bailiff into a deep salmon pool when caught attempting to extract a fish supper. The 'squad' was completed by a light heavyweight, 'Dodger' MacHardy, who had been a fairground pug, and myself, selected purely for my 6 feet 2 inches and 12 stone, but with complete disregard for my inclination to avoid bloodshed at any costs.

The big night was a home match, held in the local corn exchange. This was a vast Victorian building, designed for quite a different purpose but large enough to accommodate an audience of a size which the stuff of West End theatre managers' dreams are made. It was packed to suffocation, the whole of the front row glittering with officers, from a visiting general downwards, in full mess kit with Boer War medals and all. Behind them in a haze of puffed Woodbines stretched rank upon rank of licentious soldiery in Number One walking-out dress. In all modesty I should mention that attendance at such events was a compulsory parade. Otherwise 90 per cent of the audience would no doubt have been much more happily occupied somewhere else.

The batting order was smallest first, which for our lot meant Dinger, then in ascending order of avoirdupois until the culminating event of the evening, the thump and thunder of the heavyweights.

I should explain here the rules governing Army boxing at that time. Applause, jeers, sneers and any other form of vocal expression were strictly limited to the entry of the gladiators, the interval between rounds (bouts were limited to three rounds of two minutes each) and the announcement of the decision. While the contestants were engaged in conflict complete silence had to be observed. There was no referee in the ring behind whom one might shelter or appeal for mercy. Instead, three ringside adjudicators, all officers, marked points. At the end of a bout the two junior officers handed their cards to the chief referee, an officer not usually below that of major, who, in the event of a disagreement, gave his casting vote.

Dinger sprang out of his corner as if his only intention was to get round to the Crown before the beer ran out. His opponent took matters more seriously, and he circled, ducked and bob-bed. By the end of the first round nobody had landed a blow. At the second bell Dinger, uninhibited by the formality of touching gloves, crossed the ring and delivered a right to the solar plexus, which had his opponent gasping scarcely before he had time to get off his canvas stool. He sat down again abruptly—it was one up to us and four to go.

Fergus Campbell was next. As he emerged from our changing room in the Gents' lavatory (the opposition, quite properly, had been given the marginally more comfortable Ladies) and clambered through the ropes, there was an explosion of enthusiastic applause. By the time the noise had died down Fergus was in his corner, wearing the red sash of the home side and scowling at his green-sashed opponent. At the bell he went in prodding and poking. The affair lasted the full three rounds and in the end the chief referee held up the red flag.

The building erupted to a stamping of feet and cheering which threatened its very structure—it was two up to us and three to go.

MacConnachie proved a disappointment. Maybe he was playing the odds from his old bookmaking days and betting against himself. But it still left us two to one up.

Dodger looked a certainty. At the end of round two he was so far ahead I abandoned the comfort of the Gents' lavatory seat and plucked up enough courage to get to the ringside to see him past the post. With three wins to us my performance would be of little importance. Then he was caught by a duck and punch that came from somewhere near his opponent's ankles and he was counted out.

Two all! I scuttled back to the safety of the lavatory seat while I awaited my call. The hall was in ferment. I was in torment.

'Ladies (what Ladies?) and Gentlemen!' (Who did the goddam Regimental Sergeant-Major think he was, a dance band announcer at the Hammersmith Palais?) 'Now for the last and final bout of the evening.'

Somehow I climbed into my corner; eight feet away in the other corner was a man-mountain—and mean-looking with it.

'Jaysus!' hissed Corporal Alfie Rhodes, the leather-faced ex-all-India Army boxing champion, who was my second, 'you've picked a right big 'un.'

'Quiet!' yelled the Sergeant-Major. In the sudden silence someone farted loudly.

'Shake hands and stand back.'

We obeyed orders.

'Box on,' demanded the Major from the safety of his umpire's chair.

I took three sharp steps backwards, right against the ropes. It was the furthest I could get.

'That's it,' urged Alfie from my corner. 'Let him come to you.'

Man-mountain came on in a rush. In a wild panic, I side-stepped possibly leaving one foot behind, with the result that he went straight through the ropes and never got back in again. He was knocked out cold.

Slowly the Major raised the red flag and then even the General was on his feet cheering and clapping.

'Dead clever stuff! Never seen anyone so fast on their feet,' said Alfie in admiration.

Next day, five minutes after reveille, it was back to the gym with my thin vest and sexy knickers. Unfortunately, I was something of a hero!

CHAPTER 3

In early 1939 the prospect of another war had not crossed our minds. However, that all was not completely well with the outside world began to filter through to we cloistered professionals with the arrival of a completely new type of intake. These were not the usual run of volunteers, most of whom it was accepted were on the run from something or another, even if it was only poverty. These were the new militiamen, ordered by government decree to give three months' military service to put the country 'at the ready' in case of another world war.

Great Heavens! It had not been all that long since we'd had the war to end all wars. Perhaps 'going for a soldier' was not just to be a matter of earning a few long service and good conduct stripes in Poona or Pondicherry before qualifying for a pension and a snug billet in the Star & Garter Homes. Perhaps I should have stayed in toothpaste after all.

However, the country was in danger and it was time for desperate measures; and this desperation led to a dramatic change in my life. From being resigned to a life as a wet-behind-the-ears apology for a soldier, I suddenly became someone of importance. The reason for this change of status was simple enough. With the sudden intake of so many civilians who did not know the difference between a tin of boot polish and a bottle of Brasso, there were not enough of the old sweats around to teach them even the rudiments of the military arts.

One day I saw my name down for Company Commander's Orders and my heart sank. Company Commander's Orders were held every morning and deliquents were marched in front of a senior officer, with a great deal of stamping of feet and barking of commands, to answer for some crime such as having dirty brasses, being late on parade, or failing to salute an officer, such offences usually attracting sentences of up to fourteen days confined to barracks. Surely nobody could have spotted me urinating behind that bush on the river bank? It was all I could think of.

At the appointed time I joined the group hanging around the orderly room. My name was the first to be called.

'145084 Private Sutherland D. Atten-shun! Quick march! Halt! Right turn! Salute the officer!'

I breathed a silent sigh of relief. I was not on a charge. If I had been, at the command 'Halt!' I would have had my hat knocked off by the Company Sergeant-Major, thus not obliging the officer to return the salute of some delinquent to whom he was about to deliver anything from a bollocking to a sentence of hard labour. As is known to everybody except Americans and film directors, a soldier only salutes with his hat on.

'I have had my eye on you, Sutherland,' said the Major, the very one who had witnessed my epic victory in the boxing ring.

'Sir,' I replied, which is the standard response when addressed by an officer.

He gazed at the frugal details of my earlier academic triumphs, which I had lately been trying hard to live down. My only reading matter at that time was the strip cartoons in the *Daily Mirror* and an occasional flick through *Tit-Bits*.

'Went to a decent school, I see. There is going to be a war, you know. They are calling up the reserve—setting up Officer Training Schools. Ever thought of taking a commission?'

'I see, Sir,' was all I could say.

'Think about it. In the meantime I am promoting you to

21

lance-corporal.' He smiled his nice smile.

'Salute the officer!' roared the Company Sergeant-Major. 'Right turn! Quick march!' With much approved stamping of boots I was quick-stepped out of the orderly room.

When I told Dinger Bell, who had become one of my closest friends in rather an unholy partnership against authority, his reaction was predictable.

'A fuckin' lance jack. Gerraffitt!'—which is the Glasgow equivalent of 'You *have* to be joking'. Then, as an afterthought, he added, 'If you think you're going to pull rank on me, you've got another think coming, you fuckin' big Fanny.'

Of all terms of abuse, to be described as a 'fuckin' big Fanny' was about as far as you could go without using the ultimate expletive: 'Bastard'—the only insult which called for immediate retribution. Once I had called a mate 'a silly bastard' in the most affectionate way and, before I knew it, had found myself pinned against the barrack-room wall with a bayonet at my throat.

A few days later my promotion appeared in Company Orders. This had two immediate effects. Firstly, in addition to my normal cosmetic routine I was burdened with the added responsibility of having to blanco a single white stripe on each arm of my uniform every day. And secondly I experienced a dramatic rise in my daily pay from two shillings and tenpence to three shillings and fourpence.

If pay in those days would appear to have been on the ungenerous side, it did not seem so to myself or any of my fellow soldiers. We grumbled, of course, particularly when penalised a day's pay for losing, say, one's knife, fork and spoon, or having stoppages made for a stolen tin of boot polish. But even with beer at only fourpence a pint it was hard to get drunk and disorderly on a couple of bob, so at least the lack of financial resources lowered the risk of a spell on 'jankers'—and it was a bloody sight better than the dole queue.

There was one occasion, however, where the element of greed, present in all of us, came perilously near to putting me in that very position. In a rare moment of filial affection I decided to telephone my mother from the single public call-box available. This meant a trunk call and the expenditure of a matter of sixpence—no small sum. It was with exasperation, therefore, that I got the connection, heard my mother answer and obeyed the request to insert the requisite coin and press button A, only to have the line go dead. In petulant protest at this not-so-minor tragedy, I hammered furiously on the coinbox, whereupon the locked drawer—the receptacle into which all contributions fell—slid open, revealing a veritable Eldorado of wealth: pennies, sixpences and even shillings, almost to overflowing. It must have added up to *pounds*.

I was at once faced with the most fearful moral quandary. Two obvious courses were open to me. The first was to fill my tight-fitting uniform pockets with as much as they could hold. The second was to run to the bar where I had left my two friends, Bill Dodds and Dinger Bell, to enlist their aid in removing the unexpected windfall and share it with them It is, I maintain, to my honour that I chose the latter course.

However, by the time I had dashed back to the bar and pantingly persuaded them to abandon their half pints and return to the scene, a matter of only a few minutes, the drawer still stood open—but empty. We gazed at it in dismay; then Bill uttered the only epithet which could adequately describe anyone capable of such blatant dishonesty: 'The thieving bastards!'

I am happy to say that the culprits, two civilians, were later apprehended by the police, helplessly drunk, their pockets still stuffed with the incriminating evidence. It could well have been us in that position and the whole incident strengthened my belief that God favours the virtuous.

It was about this time that war was declared. I, however, had local problems of my own far removed from such remote distractions, and even to the hardened veterans it had little more impact than if somebody had observed that the natives were getting restless. Indeed, my uppermost feelings were only those of resentment that Hitler, Chamberlain and company had brought about a change in what had become an almost comfortable life-style.

I had become acclimatized, and even happy, in my role as mentor to young militiamen on such weighty military matters as achieving the exact patina on the toe-cap of an ammunition boot or the correct use of the button-stick so that buttons could be brightly burnished without impregnating the serge jacket with Brasso. As to my own kit, I paid Corporal Alfie Rhodes a shilling a week out of my occasional private income to keep every piece up to the highest required Army standards.

Now, quite suddenly, we were thrown into frenzied activity, learning new skills. The bayonet in its shining black scabbard was no longer an instrument of adornment for inspection on guard duty but had become overnight an offensive weapon which, affixed to the end of a .303 rifle, was, at the command 'Charge!', used to assault and grievously harm sacks of straw hanging in rows from an improvised gallows.

''Twas the bayonet won the last war, laddies,' Sergeant Corker exhorted us, 'and it will bloody-well win this one. Fix bayonets! Charge! Kill! Kill!'

We fixed; we charged; and the sacks never answered back.

There was another development which I and my fellow professional rankers found equally, if not more, alarming. When we had had our first kit issue, it had included a clip of five dummy .303 bullets, which we ensured were highly polished when duly laid out with our other accoutrements at the weekly barrack-room inspection.

Now we were issued with *live* ammunition; not to keep and

polish, but for use on a real rifle range. Our trusty .303 rifles, for so long lovingly polished and oiled, suffered the indignity of having to be loaded and the trigger pressed. Amazingly, they worked, although the destination of the bullet varied dramatically according to the age of the weapon and the ability of its operator.

Another bad sign was that officers, previously seen on official occasions only or checking out of barracks dressed up to the nines for a night out on the tiles, suddenly appeared clad in battledress to fix bayonets and let off rifles with the rest of us.

While we had grown used to the influx of militiamen, the arrival, as my Company Commander had predicted, of the reservists presented all manner of problems. Not least was their eagerness to prove that they had forgotten more about military skills than any of us rookies were ever likely to learn, combined with a delight that circumstances had enabled them to exchange the despotism of family life for the comparative freedom of Army discipline.

It was this heady intoxication on the part of one reservist in particular which caused me to be involved in a situation of some embarrassment.

If, up to this point, I have given the impression that I was happy as I had never been before in my life, it would only be partly true. And while I had no better friends in the world at that time than Bill and his brother, Piper Sandy Dodds, Dinger Bell, Alfie Rhodes and others of our little group, there were times, I must confess, when I felt the need to escape from the immediate cut and thrust of barrack-room life. So occasionally, when a letter from home enclosed a small fortune in the shape of a note of the realm, instead of immediately sharing the unexpected windfall, I would rather disloyally take myself off to a quiet communion in the cocktail bar of the local county hotel. There, in solitary state, I would enjoy a glass of dry sherry with biscuits and try to make an impression on the only female in my life, Effie, a buxom barmaid of some thirty summers, whose attitude towards me was one of tolerant motherliness.

It was, thus, that one evening I found myself alone, seated at the bar on a high stool, sipping my wine, nibbling the odd dry biscuit and exchanging pleasantries with Effie. That very morning I had been informed that my name had been put forward for a commission and Effie was obviously the person to consult before taking such a momentous decision.

Effie's bar was a sort of snuggery and opened through a hatch into the public bar, which was crowded four-deep with clamorous soldiery, quaffing great quantities of ale. In the rare event of some more exotic drink such as sherry or even a cocktail being required, the order would be retailed through the hatch via Effie, but largely we were undisturbed, her bar having long lost the patronage of the higher echelons of society for whom it had been expressly designed.

I was, therefore, somewhat dismayed when on that very evening our quiet *tête-à-tête* was disturbed by the entry of a reservist, whose leering and scruffy appearance indicated without any shadow of a doubt that he was in an advanced stage of intoxication. Effie gave him a look which would have daunted anyone not drunk beyond the bounds of belief.

'D'yo no mind of me, Effie?' he slurred, lurching forward to the bar like a man breasting the tape at the end of an Olympic marathon.

Effie was taking an order at the hatch and I could see she was making up her mind on how to deal with the intruder.

'She knows me fine,' he confided in me. 'I used to do her regular. Is that not so, Effie?'

Effie held her tongue but even with her back turned I could hear the ominous sound of her tightly-laced corsets cracking as she occupied herself with filling the glasses.

At this lack of response, our hero climbed on to the brass rail and, taking a rather limp object out of his trousers, slapped it on the counter—or rather it fell out with a soft plop.

'If ye didna remember me face, maybe ye'll remember that,' he announced triumphantly.

Effie turned, a tray of drinks in her left hand, and as she passed on her way to the hatch, picked up a small fork from a plate of cocktail sausages with which on her way past she deftly skewered the offending object to the counter.

Never have I heard such screams of agony and outrage. As the victim writhed in agony on the floor, I sat frozen to my stool, wondering what on earth I should do. Obviously the situation called for some sort of initiative. Fortunately my dilemma was resolved by the arrival of two of his mates from whom he had become separated, and they carried him out, wailing, into the night.

The worry from my point of view was that the matter would be reported to the authorities and I would be named as a witness, if not a participant, in this bizarre incident. A sergeant in the Military Police, who arrived on the scene shortly after, warned me that I might be required to give evidence at the almost inevitable court martial—not at all the sort of situation in which a potential future officer and gentleman should find himself.

While worrying about the possible ramifications of Effie's demonstration of incisive armed attack, a number of factors were beginning to persuade me that perhaps there were advantages, particularly in times of war, in holding the King's Commission. Not the least of these was that it appeared to me that, while we poor infantry spent all our time on foot, officers were frequently to be seen riding in motor cars and that when it came to 'Fix Bayonets. Charge!', it was, for a change, the lower ranks who were first in line.

There was also the matter of my boxing career, since at about this time I found myself, due to an unhappy series of accidents, the unwilling finalist in the Command Heavyweight Championship. A couple of likely lads had been posted to the BEF at the eleventh hour, thus giving me an unwanted walkover, and another had called off, pleading a painful attack of piles, which I regarded as a pretty unfair excuse. I did, I must confess, score a couple of victories against marginally smaller and more terrified opposition, but these did nothing to engender the slightest confidence of success against my brother finalist, whose record in the other half of the seedings had been impressive. Worst of all, through lack of any other form of diversion on our cabbage patch, the Command Championships were being billed as the highlight in the list of forthcoming events.

With this near-unto-death sentence hanging over my head

and the date fixed for my departure to join the Officer Cadet Training Unit—OCTU in Army parlance or 'Up-You' in the vocabulary of Dinger Bell—two days later, I was saddled with yet a further unwelcome responsibility.

We had in my barrack room—God only knows how he got there—a young Cockney called Runcorn. Now, if there is one thing likely to set a man apart from his fellows, particularly in a Scottish regiment, it is the matter of accent. Even to talk 'Geordie' was a thing to be made mock of, although from our camp Tyneside was geographically closer than Edinburgh. To talk with a Cockney accent was quite unheard of—it was almost as bad as talking 'posh', which was an affectation reserved solely for commissioned officers. The other side of the coin, of course, was that for an officer to have a regional accent was quite unacceptable to his fellows. Fortunately in this respect I was bi-lingual.

But Private Runcorn's troubles were not confined to matters of pronunciation. He was also dreadfully homesick, given to wracking sobs after lights-out, and was a compulsive bed-wetter. However, perhaps the greatest cross that he had to bear was his appearance. He was an albino, covered all over in almost transparent downy white hair.

In all forms of community life, from schooldays onwards, and indeed even in family life, there are the dominators and the dominated, the bullies and the bullied. And almost the worst characteristic of this deplorable aspect of human nature is the readiness with which the bullied will join forces with the bullies and become the worst tormentors if a common victim can be found who will distract attention from their own vulnerability.

In the role of victim Runcorn was a natural. Not an evening in the barrack room was complete without his being paraded naked for the delight of the spectators, and every morning he would awake from a restless sleep to find that someone had urinated in his boots. Not surprisingly, the barrack room woke up one morning to find that Runcorn had gone on the run.

As far as we saw it, his only hope was that somehow he might make it back to his native London and get lost in the teeming blacked-out capital. But with his distinctive appearance and lack of guile, no one expected that he would get very far. It was with no surprise, therefore, that within twelve hours it was reported that he had been arrested in Glasgow, where he was languishing in Barlinnie Prison, awaiting collection by a military escort.

There were few of our lot who were not aware of the agony of Private Runcorn, and I like to think that there were many, apart from myself, who had hoped that somehow he would make it clear away. I therefore felt that fate had dealt me an unkind blow when I learned that I was detailed to be the NCO in charge of the escort, and little comforted to be told that Dinger was to be my companion. Dinger had many characteristics to recommend him as a fellow mucker in the daily rough and tumble of Army life, but I had never thought of sensitivity and compassion as amongst his more obvious virtues.

We were to travel to Glasgow, stay overnight, collect the prisoner at first light next day and then return to camp by the earliest train. It was with a heavy heart that I collected the travel warrant from the orderly room—and a pair of handcuffs. Dinger's reactions were somewhat different.

'Grand. Jist grand,' he enthused. 'We'll hae a great night out wi' ma pals. Jist you see. You won't have to put your hand in yer pocket. Drink, man: ye'll droon in it!'

Certainly the first part of Dinger's prediction proved true. He insisted that we should ignore the opportunity of a bed for the night in an Army barracks. Instead we were to put up at his mum's. Mum Bell—and so far as I could see at first sight at least ten other Bells of various sexes, ages and relationships—resided in what was known as a 'single-end' in a Gorbals tenement block.

The gaunt Victorian tenements of the Gorbals district, each with a cold-water sink and a lavatory shared between four 'single-ends' on the stone-staired half-landings, have long since been reduced to rubble and in their place high-rise office blocks and factory buildings have mushroomed on the site they once occupied, hard by the muddy waters of the Clyde. In 1940, however, they housed a section of society that was deplored—by reputation—for its drunken, dissolute and generally anti-social way of life. But for warmth and loyalty to their 'ain folk' I have yet to meet their equal.

The evening passed in a blur of pints and half bottles produced from back pockets as we lurched from pub to pub, arms linked in full song. 'We're Going to Hang out the Washing on the Siegfried Line', 'Run, Rabbit, Run', and 'Knees up Mither Broon' were interspersed with the inevitable 'I belong to Glasgae'—which was certainly going 'roond and roond' by the time we staggered up three double flights of stairs and collapsed in whatever space we could find amongst the great tribe of Dinger's relations.

In what seemed only ten minutes or so we reluctantly woke up, scrambled over sleeping bodies, brewed up in a blackened pot on the hob over the open fire for mugs of strong tea, scraped our chins with a shared razor and found ourselves out in the street, along with the dustbins and the foraging alley cats, while gusts of wind stirred papers greasy with the oil of the previous night's fish suppers.

I thought of Private Runcorn waiting in his cell for the clatter of keys which would herald his transfer from one place of incarceration to another. Perhaps he would be looking forward to a spell in the glasshouse and a cell of his own? But only perhaps.

'If that bugger's late, I'll murder him, so I will,' Dinger muttered, peering up the empty gas-lit street.

'What bugger?' I asked.

31

'Hammy,' came the curt reply.

I vaguely remembered Hammy from the night before—a big, slow-moving man with a gut on him like a prize sow.

Just at that moment a truck rumbled into sight, slowed and stopped.

'In,' snapped Dinger.

We both climbed into the front of the cab. Hammy let in the clutch and we ground our way off over the cobbles, the whole vehicle shuddering as we hit the tramline intersection. Nobody said a word. Half an hour later we drew up outside what I took to be Barlinnie which, even compared to Alcatraz, must have come near the top of the league for stark, brooding menace.

'Wait down the Cross,' said Dinger to Hammy as we climbed out. In my agitation and general misery I nearly forgot the handcuffs.

They had Runcorn waiting for us in a grimy room, his transparent hair matted and his eyes red as a ferret's, while his white eyelashes were damp and almost invisible.

'Had any breakfast?' I asked, just for want of something to say. He nodded listlessly.

'Sign here,' said a wooden-faced warder. I signed for one private soldier.

'Got the cuffs?'

Dinger snapped one on Runcorn's wrist, the other on his own.

Two minutes later we were out in the street again.

'What now?' I enquired of Dinger.

'I thought you were the fuckin' lance jack?' he said. 'Come on, you.' He pulled at Runcorn's handcuffed arm and we shambled two blocks down the street, where we found Hammy pulled up in an alley.

'Got the keys?'

'The what?'

'The fuckin' keys.' He tapped the handcuffs.

I handed them over. He unlocked them, leaving the whole apparatus dangling from his right wrist.

He turned to Runcorn. 'Get in there, you great Nana, behind they sacks.'

The back of the truck was filled with what looked like bags of potatoes. For a moment Runcorn gazed at Dinger with dead eyes. Then slowly some sort of comprehension stirred. Half backing away, he started to climb hesitantly over the tailboard as if fearful of some diabolical trick.

'Here,' said Dinger, as he took some screwed-up notes from his tunic and shoved them into Runcorn's hand. 'From some of the lads, and keep your bloody head down till you reach the Smoke—understand?'

Runcorn nodded but he didn't say anything.

Dinger banged the side of the lorry. 'Get fuckin' moving,' he shouted.

As the truck set off down the road, from the back I saw a pale hand flutter briefly like a white moth.

'First stop London,' said Dinger, 'I hope.' Then he felt in his pocket. 'Lend us a pound will ya. The bugger's cleaned me oot.'

'Be my guest,' I said willingly, handing over one of my last two notes.

Of course, there was a hell of a row when we got back to barracks.

'You going for an officer,' the RSM snarled at me, his black moustache quivering and his silver-knobbed swagger stick beating the air. 'You couldn't run a French letter stall in a brothel.'

Dinger took most of the blame. He had the story off pat.

'The laddie wanted the toilet on the train. Catch me in there with him, wiping his arse with me other hand. Not bleedin' likely. Must have squeezed out of the window. Like an eel he was. Probably broke his neck. Why don't you go and have a look?'

It just about got us by, but the Company Commander was far from pleased.

'Not a good start, Sutherland,' he said, shaking his head. 'Not a good start at all.'

Two years later, on leave in London, I was descending the escalators of Green Park underground station. On the up escalator passed a bowler-hatted, smartly dressed businessman engrossed in his morning paper. But there was no mistaking Runcorn's ghostly face and colourless hair.

Meanwhile, in a state of both physical and nervous exhaustion induced by the Runcorn incident, I had only three days to prepare myself for my big fight on the Saturday night. The following Monday, all being well, I would be off to prove that I had the initiative, character and power of leadership which would set me apart from the common herd—an example and an inspiration to all those who might have the good fortune to serve under me. So I decided that in the circumstances a supreme effort was called for if I stood any chance of launching myself into the higher echelons of military command with my head held high.

I can still recall the electric atmosphere of that great hall where the contest was to take place. In view of the importance of the occasion it was held on neutral ground so that the partisanship of the crowd could not be said to affect the outcome. The ring had been set in the middle of the auditorium with banks of spectators on all four sides, the contestants making their entry down a long gangplank from the dressing rooms beyond. Like real boxers we wore dressing gowns and towels over our heads like monks' cowls.

Before my big moment arrived I sat in the room I shared with a number of others, almost asphyxiated by the smell of camphorated oil and armpits, and listened to the distant sounds of the preliminary bouts.

Alfie Rhodes, my trusty second, had invented a new type of home-made jockstrap, consisting largely of cardboard, for which he claimed magically protective properties. But as soon as I had manoeuvred it into place under my shorts, it slipped down my leg and had to be abandoned at the last minute. Preoccupied with such distraction as these, my turn to run the gauntlet seemed to come mercifully soon.

As I climbed into the ring, I felt a moment of what might almost have passed for exaltation, induced, no doubt, by the roars of the spectators, the fussing of the seconds, all the paraphernalia of buckets, sponges and gumshields, and the ritual inspection of bandaged fists and gloves to ensure the absence of lethal weapons.

Then came the moment of truth.

'Seconds out of the ring,' commanded the umpire. 'Quiet, please!'

As the crowd fell obediently silent, I slipped out of my dressing gown and in the approved manner performed a little bit of a soft-shoe shuffle on the spot. Then for the first time I glanced at the opposite corner. My opponent, his back to the ring, was in the process of slipping out of a magnificent silk robe. He let it fall with a fine theatrical flourish, then, grasping the ropes, he flexed his rippling muscles before turning to raise his arms in a gesture of imperious benediction. His skin was as black and lustrous as polished jet.

When we were summoned to the centre of the ring to receive the referee's mandatory instructions—'box fair, no holding, no hitting below the belt and no eye gouging'—he fixed his eyes on me with all the detached interest of an undertaker measuring up a client for a coffin.

We touched gloves and battle commenced. Alfie and I had decided on new tactics. No tip and run, which had been my practice in the past, but rather the Dinger Bell tactic—wop 'em good and hard, preferably when they weren't ready. I took a

half-step forward, feinted with my left and brought my right across to the chin with every ounce of weight I could summon. The punch never landed, brushed aside with an almost contemptuous glove. I remember the briefest flash of white teeth and then someone was bending over me, gently raising a reluctant eyelid.

'It's all right,' I heard a voice say. 'He's coming round. I saw his eyes flicker.'

Alfie's leathery features drifted into focus: I was back in the dressing room.

Then a great black hand ruffled my hair: 'Man, you sure moved the wrong way that time.' The brown eyes were warm and friendly. I smiled back weakly.

'Not good, Sutherland,' I could almost hear the Company Commander's voice. 'Not good at all.'

However, there was an unexpected ray of sunshine when I

reported for my papers at Company office next day.

'One thing,' said the Company Sergeant-Major. 'Your pal the flute player. We won't need your evidence after all. Pleading guilty.'

'My pal the flute player?'

'The bloke who Effie done. The medics patched 'im up as best they could but they still call 'im the flute player.'

The penny dropped.

'You mean I don't have to give evidence after all?'

'That's right. Good luck . . . Sir.' He raised one eyebrow and his lips parted in the wry grin of an old soldier for whom life holds no more surprises.

CHAPTER 4

Few great military careers could have started more inauspiciously.

The only visible evidence of being in the transcendental state of metamorphosis from 'Other' to 'Commissioned' rank was that embryo officers were stripped of all evidence of any rank earned on a lower plane of existence and acquired instead a white band on their headgear and a white strip on their epaulettes. In more practical terms this meant that I had to remove my single lance-corporal's stripe and purchase, at some considerable expense, a length of white crêpe. Although a 'housewife' (pronounced 'hussif' and consisting of a pack of needles and thread, scissors, pins, a thimble, and God knows what else besides) was—just as much as a field-marshal's baton—carried in every soldier's knapsack, I had never mastered the use of it.

Thus, the task being quite beyond my capabilities, my last evening before travelling a few miles up the coast to Dunbar, where my academy of instruction was situated, was spent in Effie's bar, cut off from my closest friends, while Effie effected the transformation. I also managed to get drunk on sherry, which Effie insisted was on the house, so that when I slipped quietly out of barracks the following morning, the tell-tale cap stuffed under my battledress blouse, I was not only still punch-drunk from Saturday night but suffering from a monumental hangover.

To say that the next three months, during which we larvae evolved by nature's mysterious process into butterflies, was an unhappy interlude in my Army career would not be strictly true. It teetered between extremes of dejected exhaustion and hysteria-inducing comedy.

The spring of 1940 was turning into a hot summer and the keener students of current military affairs were showing considerable concern over the misfortunes which had overtaken our efforts to 'hang out our washing on the Siegfried Line'. The retreat from Dunkirk was much in the news at the time but it passed largely over our heads, more concerned as we were with avoiding at all costs the ultimate ignominy of being returned to our units as 'unsuitable officer material'.

This obsession with failure was something which was contracted—rather like chickenpox—after only the briefest contact with one's fellow alumni. Suddenly, for even the most lukewarm of aspirants to officer status, the letters RTU assumed a menacing significance which is hard to describe. To be Returned To Unit was to rate as low in standards of acceptability as 'Unfit for Human Consumption'.

I do not now quite know what I had expected. Perhaps a little guidance on grand strategy lest a field-marshal should fall dead at my feet and I should be required to grasp his baton like the Olympic torch. Or, less ambitiously perhaps, a few hints on which way to circulate the port after dinner on mess nights.

Instead, most of the first fortnight of the precious three months of high endeavour was devoted to cross-country running and instruction on how to recognize the first symptoms of venereal disease. 'If you feels like you're pissing broken glass, you've got gon. If you've got a bloody great chancre on the end of it, you've got syph.'

39

This was followed by an inordinate amount of rifle drill—sloping arms, presenting arms, reversing arms for military funerals and such like occasions—for which my experience as a ranker stood me in good stead. However, this seemed a somewhat strange activity since, once commissioned, we would be required to surrender our rifles forever and thereinafter depend for our protection entirely on a 0.38 revolver, quite one of the most useless weapons ever devised and infinitely less effective than the assegai or the spears of the Impi, as our grandfathers had discovered to their cost in the Zulu Wars.

The rest of the course consisted of a great deal of rushing up and down hills storming imaginary enemy positions, much marching and counter-marching, and endless physical training on the foreshore. Presumably the idea was that we should not ask our men to do something we were incapable of doing ourselves—not at all what I had in mind at the outset.

As the weeks wore by we were given a tantalizing taste of the prize so nearly in our grasp. Each Sunday evening a few names selected from among our number would be posted on the notice board. For the following week these favoured individuals would be given the opportunity to act out the fantasy of holding a commission, sporting the insignia of rank in cloth 'pips' worn on the shoulder. They were privileged to perform such vital tasks as taking morning parade or marching us off to the dining-hall. It was a great honour to be selected and an almost certain indication that one was in no danger of being ignominiously returned unwanted to the unit. It also carried the implied promise that one would pass out with a high grading and a good report. This, in turn, meant that when the time came to select the regiment one would most like to join, it was probable that one's wish would be granted.

Under these circumstances it was understandable that every Sunday evening, about the time when the appointments for the following week were due to be posted, there was quite a crowd of ambitious cadets hanging around the notice-board, trying to look casual and disinterested. My own group of particular friends studiously avoided any such exhibition of naked ambition. Instead, we made a point of signing out for the evening and took ourselves off to the golf club, where we would play a rubber or two of bridge and consume more than our ration of whisky. We were able to indulge ourselves in this latter respect because one of our number was, in civilian life, a distiller of a very high quality and well-known brand of what we Scots so aptly call 'the water of life'.

Our routine sometimes varied due to another valued friend who was director of a provincial chain of theatres. He would invite the prettiest actresses who happened to be playing in one of his theatres in Edinburgh to dine on Sunday evening and, being a true comrade, would usually ask us to join the party. I remember in particular a creature of peerless beauty who, it was reported, bathed each morning in asses' milk for the sake of her complexion and for good measure brushed her teeth with champagne. Her name was Diana Napier and I fell in love with her at first sight. The fact that she was married to Richard Tauber, then at the height of his singing career, did nothing to quench my lust.

Diana Napier certainly made me forget any hankering I may have had for my old friend Effie, so that when I managed to fix a date with her for one Sunday afternoon all on my own, my euphoria carried me through the few intervening days on gossamer wings. It was also an assignation which came gift-wrapped with the seeds of near disaster.

It so happened that the week of my date with Diana was also the week in which, to my astonishment, I had been posted to be acting Platoon Commander—the highest rank and the greatest honour of all. I had almost despaired of any recognition of my future potential as an officer, especially since, one after another, most of my closest friends had been recognized to one degree or another. The most that I felt I could look forward to was decent obscurity so that my more obvious deficiencies would not be discovered until it was too late. This sudden elevation came to me and, indeed, to all my intimates as nothing less than what the French describe so graphically as '*un coup de foudre*'. Actually, I thought I had done rather well that week and so it was with all the confidence of a man who knows his foot is on the first rung of the ladder leading to the stars that I met Diana off the train.

Dunbar, or any small Scottish township for that matter, was not exactly fun-packed, especially on a Sunday afternoon, but it did possess a rather splendid swimming pool. The day was warm, almost hot, and so the pool seemed the obvious place to dally awhile and perhaps share the odd intimate ice-cream soda.

Finding a suitably shady corner to protect the goddess's milk-white skin, the time passed rather more than pleasantly. As we strolled back to the changing cabins, Diana caught sight of a bronzed male body posed carefully on the diving board like some sort of Charles Atlas.

'Christ!' she remarked in ladylike tones which echoed round the pool. 'Who does that bloody pouf think he is?' I took one glance and followed it with a quick header into the water. Unfortunately I could not stay submerged for ever and when I surfaced I saw the beady eye of my Company Commander fixed upon me with a cold stare from the diving board.

Next day my name was posted for Company Orders.

The Company Commander, now more formally attired, was seated behind his desk. As I was marched in he glared at me in a decidedly unfriendly fashion.

'It has been reported to me, Sutherland,' he said, 'that your week as Platoon Commander has fallen short of what might be expected of a future officer. Very far short indeed.'

There was only one course of action. Bluff it out.

'I'm sorry to hear that, Sir. May I ask the nature of my deficiencies?'

For a moment he looked rather nonplussed.

'Untidy bed space.' That was one of the most damning of all sins. 'Er, slackness on parade.' He waved a hand airily. It was enough for instant RTU. 'Lack of responsibility.'

'I am afraid, Sir,' said I, looking him straight in the eye, 'I did spend Sunday afternoon by the swimming pool, but I was off duty.' I had learned that he spent *every* afternoon at the swimming pool.

There was a long silence. Then he said, 'I should return you to your unit but I am prepared to give you one more chance. Dismiss!'

After this last-minute reprieve I still had one month of my training to go, and I worked like a navvy. Whenever there was an outdoor exercise, I was the first to volunteer to carry the anti-tank rifle. I searched assiduously for officers I could salute smartly. I even turned down an invitation to dine with Charlie's most recent actress.

Then came the blessed day when we were called to the assembly hall and informed that we had passed. All that remained was for us to be fitted for our uniforms and fill in a form stating our choice of regiment.

'Congratulations, gentlemen,' concluded the OCTU Commander, whom we were to see for the first and last time of the whole course.

Charlie, Ronnie our whisky friend, myself and Puggie Price, the other member of our bridge four, decided we would try to stick together. We had to state our first, second and third choices of regiment, so we all put down the same names. These were, in order of preference, the Royal Scots, the Black Watch and the Gordon Highlanders, all of which had been commanded at some time in the distant past by one or other of our relations.

At the final parade we filed up to receive our confidential reports and be informed of our grading, which was pretty straightforward: 'A' forecast a brilliant military career; 'B' anticipated that you should at least be able to hold your end up amongst real officers and gentlemen; 'C' meant you were readily expendable and carried with it a sort of built-in apology to whichever unit one happened to be posted.

Charlie got an A and a posting to the Royal Scots.

Ronnie got an A and a posting to the Royal Scots.

Puggie got an A and a posting to the Royal Scots.

Mrs Sutherland's little boy Douglas got a C and a posting to the King's (Liverpool) Regiment.

The confidential report on my military prospects was confined to one succinct comment: 'Should be popular in the mess.'

Not a word about all the anti-tank rifles I had hauled about—or my well-polished buttons. Still, I suppose it was better than nothing.

For those who have not experienced the sartorial transition from the lowest form of non-commissioned military life to the lowest form of commissioned military existence, I can assure you that it is far more devastating than might be expected, perhaps comparable to the feelings of a young bride when, having thrown off the trappings of her maidenhood, she emerges for the first time before the public gaze in all the splendour of her going-away outfit. Indeed, I felt sure that the gilt pip on each shoulder seemed as obtrusively eye-catching as any engagement or wedding ring.

Admittedly we were able to avoid the embarrassment of being showered with confetti or knocked senseless with lucky horseshoes, but waiting for the up-train to Edinburgh, which of one accord Charlie, Puggie, Ronnie and I had selected as the natural rendezvous for our celebration, we paced the platform with much the same anxiety a spy might feel of having his disguise penetrated by some foolish slip, like a nun detected wearing ammunition boots. And when the train did arrive, Ronnie made just the sort of mistake which has led to the unmasking of many a traitor. Unthinkingly, he opened the carriage door of a third-class compartment and would undoubtedly have boarded it were it not for a bit of quick action by Puggie Price. Ronnie had simply forgotten that we were now first-class citizens.

Once in the cultural capital of the North, my recollections of the following few hours are necessarily vague. However, I do remember Charlie, who as an Edinburgh man had set himself up as the authority on the city's nightlife, declaring, as, one by one, various licensed premises ran out of drink, that there was a night club, known as the Hanover, where it was rumoured beer could be obtained after eleven o'clock. For some time we staggered about the blacked-out streets in a vain attempt to locate this miraculous oasis. Finally, at the top of Leith Walk, I spotted the slight figure of a girl in a doorway.

'Excuse me,' I enquired politely. 'Can you possibly direct us to the Hanover Club?'

'I dinna ken,' she answered. 'Y'see, I'm jist a wee sixpenny whoor.'

Although at this distance in time the offer must have appeared at least a financially attractive proposition, as a prospect for the continuation of the night's revels it offered no great appeal.

So, crossing her palm with silver, we went our various ways, swearing eternal friendship. We never met again. My three friends were killed in the same action eighteen months later. Perhaps I might not have made it either if Diana had not spoiled my prospects of military glory that afternoon by the swimming pool.

CHAPTER 5

If at the conclusion of the last chapter I have given the impression that my career as an officer cadet had been less than glorious, I will not have misled the reader. However, to give the impression that my failure to gain acceptance by the First of Foot, the Royal Scots, showed any lack of judgement on their part, would be as unfair as to suggest that to be accepted by the King's (Liverpool) Regiment was any less an honour. Also, creating such an impression would be to risk a well-deserved kick up the bottom from such comrades in arms in the King's as still survive, including those who remain amongst my closest friends.

The initial shock of learning of my posting sprang simply from my knowledge of the cross which my fellow comrade in the KOSBs, Private Runcorn, had had to bear by being pitchforked as a Cockney into a haystack of hairy Scots. What awful fate could I expect at the hands of the Sassenachs as a barbarian who had never even become civilized enough to wear knickers under his tartan skirt, let alone as one who had never seen the Blackpool Tower? As it turned out, my apprehension proved quite unfounded.

Before joining my regiment, a spell of leave reunited me with my family. My elder brother, by the simple expedient of lunching with the Colonel of the Regiment, had become an

officer in the Gordon Highlanders and was assing around in a kilt. My mother was having hysterics over disinfecting evacuee children from Glasgow of non-existent bugs. Lizzie, who had been with us for over forty years, was as usual on the point of giving notice, and old Clark, the gardener, had taken to keeping a loaded shotgun by the front door of his cottage in case there should be a repetition of the occasion when a German aeroplane had been seen to pass overhead on its way to the Orkney Islands.

To complete the happy family unit, my younger brother had developed symptoms of typhoid, as he always did at the approach of a new school term. Otherwise, as summer turned to autumn, all was about as normal as it ever would be at Castle Sutherland, while I waited patiently for details of my posting.

I was just beginning to think that perhaps my file had been lost when one of those OHMS letters which were to become such a familiar feature of my life arrived. I had been posted to a place called Wathgill, which, from close examination of a large-scale map through a powerful magnifying glass, appeared to be a minuscule area in the midst of the Yorkshire moors.

'Probably a hutted camp, old boy,' said my elder brother cheerfully. 'Cold showers. Outside bog. All that sort of thing.'

As I looked out of the drawing-room window across our suddenly attractive valley, a few flakes of snow started to fall. I shivered as I felt the first unmistakable symptoms of typhoid.

I got off the train at Richmond station, where there was no sign of the transport I had been given to expect would be waiting to meet me. Down Yorkshire way they appeared to take their snow far more seriously than in the Highland glens of home. It was blowing a blizzard and getting dark. Through the gloom I discerned three other muffled figures lugging kitbags, suitcases and sundry paraphernalia. One of them even had a bag of golf clubs. When we had gathered in the bare gaslit waiting-room on the deserted platform I soon learned we were all bound for the same destination. One of them came from Somerset, another from outside London and the third hailed from Newcastle. For them, as for me, it was their first posting, and I was pleased to discover that none of them had ever seen the Blackpool Tower nor even been through the Mersey Tunnel.

There was a general feeling that, as young officers, we ought to be showing some sort of initiative. So we decided upon the fiendishly clever plan of seeking out information as to our eventual destination from the landlord of the local hostelry—if such person and place could be found in the darkness which had now descended with arctic finality.

Ten minutes later we thankfully pushed our way through a carefully blacked-out doorway into a surprisingly snug and cheerful bar parlour. There were no other customers—only the landlord polishing glasses behind what seemed to be, for wartime, a finely stocked bar.

'You gentlemen for the camp then?' he enquired. Conscious of the need for the utmost security and of the posters on the wall announcing that 'Walls have ears' and 'Careless talk cost lives', we admitted cautiously that it was a possibility.

'Hey, mate,' shouted the landlord. 'Your lot has just shown up.'

In response a figure appeared from the rear quarters, pulling a sweat-stained side hat over his tousled hair. His battledress tunic was unbuttoned and his trousers appeared to be kept up by a piece of rope tied round his middle.

'Train on time then?' he asked. 'Truck's outside back.'

I suppose in any well-produced pantomime this, my first meeting with Private Bolton, would have been given the theatrical emphasis it deserved by a clashing of cymbals, puffs of coloured smoke and flashes of stage lightning. As it was, none of us asked why the bloody hell he had not been at the station. Instead, humping our own baggage, we all filed out meekly and piled into the back of a 15-cwt truck, whilst Bolton settled himself comfortably in the driver's seat with the engine running to keep him warm.

It is something of a wonder how anyone managed to drive at all at night with the blackout regulations then in force. Headlights were fitted with a cowl on top so that no light whatever could possibly be seen from above, whilst the glass itself was entirely covered with black paper, in the centre of which the tiniest of crosses had been cut. The amount of light thus permitted to be shown was far less than that emitted from one of those pencil torches used by boys to read naughty books under the blankets in bed after 'lights out'. This handicap, however, in no way affected the performance of Private Bolton, who plunged through the blackness as if he was determined to win the Le Mans grand prix.

By the time we pulled up in front of a long wooden hut, which turned out to be the officers' mess, only the rutted tracks of previous vehicles broke the flat plain of snow about a foot deep all around.

The mess itself was empty save for the Mess Sergeant. All the other officers were changing for dinner. He consulted a sheet on the inevitable green baize notice-board.

'Lieutenants Routledge and Sutherland, tent number eleven. Lieutenants Holt and Hogan, tent twelve.'

Tents! It had to be some traditional regimental jargon handed down from the days of the Punjab, meaning bungalows or something similar.

Unfortunately, its meaning was only too literal. Huts were in evidence, but they were for the use of other ranks. For us: two officers to one bell tent. And that was how, high up on the Yorkshire moors, we spent three months of the coldest winter in living memory. Many were the occasions when I felt like remarking to my tent mate, more in earnest than in jest: 'I am just going outside, and may be some time.'

50

Oddly enough, it was not so bad until the snow started to melt and the frost set in with a vengeance. Then every beetle and bug, field mouse or black rat sought refuge in our tents as being just marginally warmer than outside. Or they were attracted by the odd edible substances, from biscuit crumbs to frozen tubes of toothpaste. One morning, when we lit our paraffin lamp, it was to find the canvas literally black with earwigs, climbing the sides and dropping off all over us.

Bolton, having finally driven his 15-cwt truck into some inaccessible hole in the middle of the moors, had been taken off driving and one morning, to the horror of George Routledge and myself, reported for duty as our batman. From that moment any attempts at order and tidiness were by mutual consent abandoned.

We officers were, it must be admitted, a rather rum lot. Few had ever had any military ambitions. Only the Colonel and the Adjutant were regular soldiers who had joined up in the piping days of peace and been through Sandhurst. I am quite sure that neither of them had ever considered the possibility of becoming involved in anything more serious than perhaps the Aldershot Tattoo, with the possibility of a bit of foreign service in some part of the Empire, which would stand them in good stead when their time came to retire and become local magistrates—and with the annual regimental reunion to look forward to each year.

Try as the regular soldier element might, with weekly compulsory mess nights where we self-consciously played rough games after dinner, hitting each other over the head with rolled up copies of *The Times*, there was not a great deal of *esprit de corps*. To tell the truth we were a little bit short on 'class' and not greatly in demand to liven up such social occasions as the local county set persisted in maintaining during that long cold season of good cheer and good will to all men.

Although all in all it was a lousy winter, the troops had, I

think, a marginally better time than we did. All they had to do was get shaved and dressed in time for morning parade, at which it was monotonously announced that the inclement weather made it unsuitable for field training and that their activities would be devoted to what was quaintly termed 'domestic economy'. This meant them spending the day lounging around in their huts, or perhaps a spell chipping the ice in the ablutions or clearing snow. Occasionally an inspection would be ordered when every soldier had to lay out his entire kit in his bed space for examination by the orderly officer of the day.

So, as the fortunes of war swayed to and fro in the Libyan desert, we spent a great part of our time ensuring that mess tins had been brightly burnished and none of our gallant band had mislaid the odd sock or had a hole in his sweater.

After fulfilling their 'domestic economy' duties, the troops were free to fraternize with the thin-on-the-ground but hospitable locals of the surrounding countryside or visit one of several pubs which were out of bounds to the officer class. Unfortunately, they socialized with an enthusiasm that resulted in due course in a considerable number of paternity suits, while we officers kept our own company.

It was a situation which could not continue indefinitely and at last one day each officer received a sealed letter, delivered by hand by an orderly room sergeant and marked 'Top Secret. Destroy immediately after reading'. My tent mate and I received our letters as we sat on our camp beds discussing, as usual, the possibility of getting the transfer we had applied for to the Libyan desert, where we were vaguely aware some of our army were enjoying tropical weather conditions.

Tearing open the envelopes with wild surmise we scanned the contents eagerly. *This could be it!*

The message was simple: 'All officers to report to the officers' mess for CO's Conference 1600 hrs today.'

As we were discussing this momentous communication, Private Bolton put his head through the tent flaps.

'Got your bits of paper then?' he remarked. 'Four o'clock officers' mess. Better not be late. The old man's in a great state of excitement.'

'How the devil do you know?' we asked in outraged unison.

'Got me spies, you know.' He tapped his nose significantly. 'We're being sent down to Geordieland to do a bit of guarding the old beaches.'

I screwed up my message and hurled it at the appalling Bolton. 'Get out!' I shouted.

I shouted 'Get out!' at Bolton most days.

When we filed into the mess it was to find it had been transformed into the sort of briefing centre seen in films about pilots going on death or glory missions over enemy territory. At one end the CO sat behind a table, looking tense and drawn, while the Adjutant messed about arranging a large blackboard. On the wall behind was pinned a large-scale map. At a distance it looked remarkably like a map of the north-east of England. With a sinking heart I suddenly knew that Bolton had got it right as usual. We were definitely not destined to join the open-necked-shirt brigade in sunny North Africa.

Our Colonel was not a bad old buffer. He must have been on the point of retirement when Hitler temporarily put paid to his plans. He had a grey walrus moustache which bristled in a rather endearing way and sported a monocle which he had a habit of screwing in and out of his eye in moments of stress such as this.

When we were all seated he began in a voice fraught with emotion. 'Gentleman, I have just come from a top secret meeting at Divisional Headquarters. I cannot of course discuss higher strategy with you at this stage but I can give you a brief outline of the perilous situation in which our country finds itself, following the serious setback suffered by our Expeditionary Forces last year. I will attempt to demonstrate the gravity of this peril in the simplest terms.'

At this point he rose, took hold of a stick of chalk held in readiness for him by the Adjutant and approached the blackboard. With a quick flourish he drew a line across the top right-hand corner and wrote in rapid strokes the word 'Germany'. Halfway through, such was his excitement, the chalk broke, but the Adjutant was at hand with a fresh piece.

As we held our collective breaths he wrote across the middle of the board 'The North Sea' and, three pieces of chalk later, in the bottom left-hand corner, 'Great Britain'. Then with a final majestic gesture he drew an arrow right across the North Sea with the sharp end pointing at what could have been Newcastle-upon-Tyne. By this time I was starting to get the hang of things and for a brief moment hopeful that in his excitement the Colonel has pointed the arrow in the wrong direction. He had not.

'The enemy is at our gates,' he announced. 'It is to be our honour, our privilege, *and our duty*, to defend our native land with the last breath in our bodies. The regiment moves at dawn to take up a heavy responsibility. It has fallen to us to defend South Shields.'

CHAPTER 6

The sudden move into what our Colonel insisted on calling the 'Front Line' had two inestimably important advantages from my point of view. Firstly, the company, of which I had quite improbably become second-in-command, managed to requisition a fairly modern bar-restaurant as an officers' mess. What had been sleeping-in sevants' quarters upstairs became our bedrooms on the ration one officer:one room. After our Himalayan winter the luxury seemed almost unreal.

The second great advantage was that eventually I found a way of dispensing with Private Bolton's services as my batman. It was not simply a matter of his treating me, as he did all authority, with the greatest disrespect. In fact, in his own sort of way I think he rather liked me. Nor was it that my Sam Browne belt and tunic buttons did not outshine those of all my fellow officers on mess nights. The trouble with Private Bolton was simply his concern that his compulsory involvement in the greatest holocaust the world had ever known should cause him the least possible personal inconvenience.

Having lost one cushy job as a truck driver, he had settled for the next cushiest as a batman, and the way he played it meant he was excused all parades and other forms of physical exercise or military training. This state of affairs drove Company Sergeant Major Kelly mad. He argued that, like everyone else, batmen should take their turn on guard duties and other tiresome chores, which they all did except Bolton. When asked to explain his absence for a duty for which he had been detailed, he would sigh lugubriously and explain, as to a child, that his officer needed him—something I would hotly deny when tackled by the ferocious SM Kelly. Like every other subaltern I was openly afraid of SM Kelly but somehow Bolton got away with it. In the end Kelly stopped protesting and Bolton continued his happy and carefree existence.

Just how happy and carefree was his life I did not realize until one afternoon, returning unexpectedly to my room and unable to find the handkerchief I had inadvertently left behind, I could not find Bolton either.

Enquiries elicited the not-too startling information that Bolton did not care for the food provided in the officers' mess: nor for that matter did any of us. Bolton, I was given to understand, lunched out every day.

On closer inspection of my quarters I realized that not only was the spare handkerchief missing but so was a great deal of my kit. Bolton, it appeared, always took it with him to lunch. And the reason why was revealed after further enquiries.

Waiting until all the officers had stumbled up the steep hill to the Company lines with haversack rations for the day, Bolton would take a leisurely stroll to the nearby house of his girlfriend, she having been acquired immediately after our arrival in the area. He would then hand over such of my kit as required attention together with any dirty washing to be done, including his own, and should the weather be sufficiently clement would spend the day on the beach we were supposed to be guarding. Then, sometime later and having partaken of a suitable lunch prepared for him, he would return with my clothes, which I invariably found neatly laid out when I got back from yet another depressing day of routine duties.

It was not the disclosure of this convenient arrangement,

57

however, which caused Bolton's eventual downfall. After all, he was only showing the initiative which we were constantly drumming into our troops was such a desirable quality and although Bolton's behaviour was outrageous it did result in my being the best turned-out officer in the regiment. So I was forced to turn a blind eye, grit my teeth and carry on with Bolton's 'services' as my batman—but not for long.

It so happened that among a recent intake of recruits was a Maltese who had been a waiter in no less august an establishment than the Savoy Hotel in London. He was small, dark, and with a not unattractive ingratiating manner. Just before the outbreak of hostilities he had acquired British citizenship.

But one thing Private Mexas was not cut out to be was a soldier. The mere sight of a rifle positively frightened the wits out of him and when required to fire the thing, the only time he managed to hit a target it was always the one two away from what he was supposed to be aiming at.

After Mexas had been with us for only a few weeks he had managed, without too much difficulty, to succeed Private Bolton as Number 1 on Sergeant-Major Kelly's list of 'horrible showers'—the SM's most dire form of abuse.

Kelly was a regular soldier of heaven knows how many years experience and, in common with most of his ilk, never spoke without shouting. A small, rotund figure with a face as red as the setting sun, he never walked, he strutted. And he never stopped strutting without stomping his feet as if on sentry duty. He was as Irish as the bogs and, improbable though it may have seemed at the time, after the first few months of our acquaintance he was to become one of my wisest counsellors and closest friends.

Just then, however, we were at something approaching loggerheads over the question of Private Mexas. It so happened that the Company Commander, a lawyer by profession, had been posted to the Judge Advocate's department where all lawyers eventually finished up prosecuting at courts martial—thus leaving it to less qualified officers, for example ex-toothpaste salesmen like myself, to represent the accused. Alarmingly, I found myself temporarily in command of the company and taking orderly room each morning, with SM Kelly marching in the offenders, roaring like a bull, stamping his boots and knocking off hats in all directions. It was a good week when he did not have Mexas up before me for some minor offence or another at least two or three times.

Then one night Mexas really pulled the big one.

I should explain here that our company, being a detachment, seldom saw our Colonel, occupied as he was with higher strategy at his HQ somewhere inland. However, he was very conscious of his responsibility to keep us on our toes, in a state of perpetual alertness and ready for the day when the Boche would appear out of the mists of the North Sea and throw his full might against our impregnable defences.

These defences consisted of rolls of barbed wire stretched across the easier approaches, such as where the cliffs were less steep, and, at regular half-mile intervals, small cement pillboxes with apertures on three sides through which a rifle could be poked. Moreover, each man had in his permanent charge five rounds of live ammunition. Part of our gun or guard duty was to man these pillboxes through the hours of darkness with a sentry posted outside with 'one up the spout' lest the odd Panzer division should creep up on us unobserved.

Now 'Joe Soap', as the Colonel was affectionately known, concerned as he was about our vigilance, had hit on a great idea. Always choosing the blackest of nights, he would drive his staff car as near to one of the pillboxes as he could without being observed. Then he and the Adjutant would get out and creep up on the sentry who, with any luck, would spot them. If not the Colonel would attract his attention by some means, such as a

stifled cough, whereupon the following dialogue was required to take place:

Sentry: Halt! Who goes there? Friend or foe?
Colonel: Friend.
Sentry: What is the password?
Colonel: 'Cock-a-doodle-doo' (or whatever).
Sentry: Step forward and be recognized.

Providing everybody stuck to the script all was fine and dandy. The trouble with this foolproof scenario was that Joe Soap would often purposely get the password wrong or say 'Foe' instead of 'Friend'. This would put the unfortunate sentry in a fearful fix, knowing quite well that he was not dealing with the long-awaited German invasion. As he hesitated Joe would lumber out of the darkness shouting 'Adjutant, put that man on a charge! Turn out the guard!'

The guard would then be treated to a lengthy harangue on the peril in which they collectively, and the sentry in particular, were placing the whole country. 'Next time,' Joe would conclude, 'I expect the sentry to shoot on sight.' Then he would disappear into the night while everyone cursed at having their sleep disturbed, but nevertheless managed to have a good laugh about the incident the following morning.

With the inevitability of a Greek tragedy, it was fated that Mexas, who was always being given extra guard duty for some misdemeanour or another, should sooner or later be the sentry on watch when Joe Soap turned up to play the time-honoured game.

Mexas started well with his 'Halt! Who goes there? Friend or Foe!'

'Foe!' cried the Colonel in a loud firm voice.

The next moment there was a most frightful explosion as Mexas let off his rifle. Of course, being Mexas, the bullet whizzed off harmlessly, eventually to plop somewhere far out in the North Sea. But the Colonel went to ground as if he had been attacked with an elephant gun. From somewhere he could be heard shouting, 'Turn out the guard! Arrest that man! Guard commander, can you hear me? *I am your Colonel!*' Mike Greenwood, who happened to be the guard commander, armed himself with a powerful torch and went off to search for Joe. He found him crouched with the Adjutant behind a large boulder and giving forth a stream of obscenities hardly fit for the ears of even the hardiest of campaigners.

The only question for debate after that was whether Mexas would be shot or only be imprisoned for life. In the event the Colonel turned up unexpectedly for a drink in the mess the following evening. After a sherry or two he took me aside, hemming and hawing while his monocle kept falling out of his eye. Then he said, 'About that affair last night. Damned good show. Bullet missed me by a whisker. Must be a crack shot. Could do with more like him. Don't want to hear of the matter again. Understand?'

'Yes, Colonel,' I said. 'Thank you, Colonel.'

I should really have said, 'Thank you, Private Mexas,' for putting such an abrupt end to the Colonel's alertness campaign.

Sergeant-Major Kelly, however, appraised the affair somewhat differently. Indeed, it only helped to increase his dislike of Private Mexas. When I remonstrated that he was picking on the fellow unfairly, Kelly's face would take on a shade of red verging on the purple, and next morning Mexas would be up before me again. My reaction was to stop giving reprimands or a few days' confined to barracks, even to dismiss the most blatant irregularities, such as failing to polish his boot studs.

When Kelly blew his top for the umpteenth time I hit upon a brilliant idea.

'Tell you what, Sergeant-Major,' I said, 'you give me Mexas

as my batman and mess waiter and you can have Bolton.'

From Kelly's reaction I suddenly knew how Salome must have felt having John the Baptist's head delivered to her on a platter.

''Tis a bargain, sorr!' he bellowed. For a moment I thought he was going to shake me by the hand. Instead he stamped his feet vigorously and saluted twice.

It did not take Bolton long to recover from the shock of his sudden return to the rigours of military routine which his comrades endured so stoically and with so little complaint. After a few head-on collisions with the Sergeant-Major and a few more entries on his 122 he developed a rather tiresome weakness in his back. (Form 122 is a record of each soldier's misdemeanors, similar to driving licence endorsements. Bolton's 122s could be shuffled like a pack of cards.) Bolton's back complaint so impressed the medical officer that he ordered him to be put on light duties only. Thus, while Kelly raged like a hungry lion deprived of its prey, Bolton sought refuge in the Quartermaster's office where his main responsibility was to make tea.

It was just after the Mexas affair that we received the most astonishing news. The Brigade Commander intended to visit our company and would be pleased to take luncheon with the officers. Truth to tell none of us knew that we were part of a brigade and a cog, however small, in so vast an organization. At OCTU I had been allowed a brief glimpse of a brigadier, red tabs and all, who was supposed to be running the show, but otherwise Joe Soap with his crown and one pip on each shoulder was the pinnacle of my knowledge of the higher echelons of Army command.

The Brigadier, who had a suitably hyphenated name, had expressed the wish that his visit should be as informal as possible and that he wanted to make the personal acquaintance

63

of some of the more junior officers under his command. On me, therefore, as acting Company Commander, would fall the honour and responsibility of chief host to this being from the military stratosphere.

I would have been a good deal more nervous were it not for the presence of Mexas. My deal with SM Kelly had proved a resounding success. Miraculously reprieved from the shadow of the firing squad and, perhaps even more miraculous from his point of view, removed from day-to-day contact with Kelly, Mexas had become a changed person. Not only did he outshine even Private Bolton's girlfriend as my personal batman but he took charge of the mess as to the manner born. Meals were served with a dexterity and a flourish which only those rich enough to patronize the Savoy Hotel could appreciate. A spoon inadvertently dropped at table and Mexas was there to replace it with a clean one; a carelessly folded newspaper was whisked away to be returned to its proper place duly ironed; a fly rash enough to intrude in the ante-room was skilfully and unobtrusively dispatched.

While rumour filtered through that Hitler's invasion fleet was ominously preparing for imminent invasion, and his bombers occasionally flew low overhead to drop their deadly cargo on more industralized targets, we strove to keep up with Mexas' exacting standards. I made him a lance-corporal and gave him responsibility not only over the mess staff but over what I grandly termed 'the wine cellar', a painstakingly collected selection of rather indifferent wines which were served on mess nights to accompany the *bully boeuf à la Mexas* as if it were nectar straight from the slopes of Mount Olympus.

Thus I faced the day of our Brigadier's visit with a certain amount of confidence. I had been closely briefed by the Adjutant. It was to be treated as a normal working day. Officers would wear battledress and return to their duties promptly at 1400 hours. The Brigadier did not approve of drinking or smoking. The Brigadier was looking for the efficiency of the unit to be reflected in the conduct of its officers. The Colonel would expect a full report of events within two hours after the departure of the Brigadier.

I discussed this with Mike Greenwood, who was next senior to me. Mike, who before his services had been enlisted to save democracy had worked as a site manager for a construction firm, did not appear to take the forthcoming event too seriously.

'You mean I can't tell him the one about what the actress said to the Bishop?'

I gave him one of my looks. 'The Adjutant says the Brigadier is a very clean-living man.'

'You mean he'll probably know it already?' said Mike in mock disappointment.

At 1245 hours precisely the Brigadier's large staff car drew up in the forecourt, pennant flying. My immediate impression of him seemed to confirm my worst fears. He was tall and lean with a world-weary face. He walked rather hen-toed and spoke in an oddly high-pitched drawl rather like a vicar announcing the next psalm.

One of my worries had been over the matter of pre-luncheon drinks. The others had been warned not to start sloshing back the beer at the slighest excuse, but it seemed highly uncivilized not to offer him anything, even if only an orange squash.

To my horror I found myself saying, 'Would you care for some refreshment before luncheon?', just like some maiden aunt who took special pride in her home-made cordial.

The Brigadier looked slightly apologetic. 'I don't suppose you have any Scotch?' he enquired.

You could have knocked us over collectively with a very small feather. My immediate instinct was that this was some sort of trap and that if one of our precious bottles was produced we'd all be reported. Should I deny that we had any of the demon drink?

Before I even had time to panic, Mexas solved my dilemma by appearing from nowhere bearing a full bottle and a siphon of soda which he placed in front of our guest.

'Ah, good old Johnny Walker,' he said, and I could almost hear his lips smacking.

Half a bottle of Johnny Walker later we went through to lunch. Two o'clock came and went unnoticed. The wine went round and round. Tom told the Brigadier what the actress said to the Bishop. The Brigadier said he had heard it before.

When the time came for him to leave he was more hen-toed than ever. In a drawl considerably more pronounced than when he had arrived, he informed us that we were a capital lot of fellows and a credit to the Brigade. Hitler would be sorry for it if he tried to land on our bit of coast.

I just about had enough wits left to send a message to HQ. It read: 'Brigadier just left. Very Happy.'

When I congratulated Corporal Mexas soon after on his contribution to the Brigadier's contentedness little did I know what the Fates had in store for us both.

A few days later I was summoned to HQ.

'About the Brigadier's visit,' said the Colonel.

'Yes, Sir,' I said, trying on my blue-eyed innocent look.

'Oddest damn thing. He wants you on his staff at Brigade HQ. You'd better read this yourself.'

He tossed over a dispatch. It read: 'Lieutenant Sutherland to be posted to 102 Brigade Headquarters soonest possible. Command new reconnaissance unit to be gazetted Temporary Acting Captain.'

All I could think of saying was 'Good God'.

'Have to get a replacement but you'd better get ready to pack your traps,' said Joe Soap, not unkindly.

I thought of the unknown hand which had written 'Should be popular in mess' on my confidential report. I hoped the Brigadier did not want me to bring my own whisky.

66

I returned to the mess to find Mexas in a high state of agitation, and he immediately asked if he could see me in private. Once in my room tears welled in his eyes. He produced from his battledress pocket a crumpled letter written in pencil on lined paper. 'Read this please,' he urged.

The contents were brief: 'Lennart is having your Maria. You come back quick.' It was signed 'A Friend'.

Mexas blurted out, 'Lennart was my good friend. I must go or they will be making babies.'

In spite of his quaint English I got the message good and strong. Mrs Mexas was having a high old time in bomb-torn London while her husband was doing his bit for King and country—even if Sergeant-Major Kelly did not appreciate his contribution to the same extent as I did.

As a matter of convention I immediately informed Kelly and told him Mexas had family troubles and must be given a few days' leave on compassionate grounds. Kelly was outraged and used one of his favourite expressions of derision.

'Compassionate leave, my Irish arse,' he shouted. 'Passionate leave more likely. Just wants a bit of tail. These ruddy Greeks or whatever he is are all the same. Can't leave it alone. Anyway, all leave has just been cancelled,' he added triumphantly.

This was unfortunately true. The higher powers were getting into such a twist about the imminent arrival of the enemy on our shores that every able-bodied soldier was required to man the ramparts.

In our sector things were being taken so seriously that sappers had begun mining the esplanade at South Shields, that is until a couple blew themselves up and the work was suspended. We'd had a bit of trouble, too, with bodies being washed ashore. This was one problem we happily handed over to the coastguard and the local police, with the inevitable quarrels as to where the ultimate responsibility lay. These bodies had a tiresome habit of turning up at a point where one authority's jurisdiction ended and another's began. It was not unknown in the more marginal cases for a body to be dragged over the boundary on one night and be returned to its original resting place on the next. It all added up to a growing realization that there was a war on and no effort was spared to impress on us the seriousness of the situation.

In the case of Private Mexas, however, I was determined that the regulations should be bent. Perhaps if my departure to fresh pastures had not been so imminent I might not have stood up to Kelly, but as it was I signed a 48-hour pass for Mexas and told the Quartermaster's office to get on with the formalities. Kelly, of course, turned bright puce and our growing appreciation of each other's qualities suffered a temporary set-back.

Mexas arrived in London and proceeded to the flat he shared in Islington with his wife. There was nobody at home so he let himself in and, worn out with fatigue and emotion, he settled down in a sitting-room armchair to wait while darkness fell over the capital.

When he awoke it was to hear voices coming from the bedroom, to which access could be gained without going through the sitting room. On investigating he saw a crack of light coming from under the bedroom door. Arming himself with his rifle, he threw the door open to reveal his erstwhile friend in bed with his wife.

Mexas did not hesitate. As the pair leapt up he fired from the hip. With a low moan his wife fell to the floor, while Mexas pursued her lover out of the door and down the stairs, letting off his rifle in his direction at intervals until Lennart gained the street and disappeared completely naked into the blackout.

As all students of crime will readily recognize, at the ensuing trial the matter of the fatal ammunition at once assumed grave importance. One of the regulations in force at the time must, like several others, have been the product of some fevered brain at the War Office. It decreed that a soldier going on leave should hand in his precious five rounds of ammunition. If on arrival at his destination he found out that there was a war going on he should at once report to the nearest unit, draw five rounds of ammunition, and throw himself into the fray.

The question that the jury had to answer was: had Mexas deliberately set out with murder in his heart and five rounds of ammunition which should have been handed in, retained specifically for that purpose? If so it was murder. If, however, through some administrative error he had not been asked to surrender his ammunition, the verdict could be one of manslaughter under the most mitigating of circumstances: the shock of the discovery of his wife's infidelity, his hot-blooded Latin temperament, the deceit of his closest friend. There would not be a dry eye in the jury box.

The Company Commander, for whom I was deputizing, happily made a reappearance at this time, and in his dual capacity as CO and as a qualified lawyer undertook the investigation.

Kelly was adamant. In the flap to get Mexas off, when the man should never have been given leave in the first place (dark looks at me), he had omitted to check in his ammunition. Therefore it was his fault and he accepted all the blame. Kelly had not the slighest doubt that Mexas was aiming at her lover when he hit and killed his wife. His record as a marksman could leave no one in any uncertainty about that.

By the time of the trial I had moved on but of course I kept in close touch. Mexas received a very light sentence and was dismissed the service. Kelly was given a severe rap over the knuckles.

Some weeks later I was discussing the matter with Mike Greenwood over a pint.

'Funny thing about the ammunition book,' he said reflectively. 'It was never found you know. Couldn't be produced in evidence.'

The ammunition book was a record of all ammunition issued and to be accounted for.

'If I follow your drift, where did Mexas get another five rounds from?'

'Next door bed space. Reported lost but Kelly got them replaced and told the bloke to shut up.'

I pondered for a while. 'Why did Kelly do it? He couldn't stand little Mexas.'

'Why don't you ask him?'

I never did.

A year or two after the war I was lunching in one of London's more fashionable restaurants. I was selecting a single pat of butter to go with the cheese—rationing was still rigorously in force—when a quiet voice behind me said 'If you require some more butter, sir, I think it could be arranged.'

'Thank you, Mexas,' I said without turning around.

CHAPTER 7

Brigade Headquarters had taken over a pleasantly spacious
country house well inland—a very different matter from being
'in at the sharp end' as the Colonel used to put it, with nothing
but a mere 400 miles of stormy sea between us and the
Germans. Pheasants strutted on the lawn and among other
amenities were a billards room and a well-stocked library.

All the officers were regular Army except the Brigadier, who
had served in the 1914–18 war and been an ardent Territorial
ever since. In private life he had been a brewer, and to say that
he was eccentric would be a gross understatement. The Brigade
Major, who briefed me in to my duties, gave me the first hint.

'One thing, Sutherland,' he warned. 'When the Sunday
papers arrive no one, *absolutely no one*, must touch the *News of the
World*. It is to be taken to the Brigadier's office straight away.'

My imagination started to boggle. Could it be that beneath
that austere exterior was all the frustrated passion of a sex
maniac? Would this deeply religious aesthete, inflamed with
drink and lust, be one day caught exposing himself to a platoon
of ATS girls? In those far-off less permissive days the *News of the
World* was notorious for its bold and detailed reporting of
sexually-motivated crime and even printed pictures and cartoons which left little to the imagination.

71

As I was to discover, the truth was, in its way, even more alarming. The paper had at that time a weekly feature by the distinguished astrologer R. H. Naylor called 'What the Stars Foretell'. Every Sunday morning the Brigade Commander would closet himself in his office with the astrologer's article spread out on his large and impressive desk. With this invaluable aid he would plot the tactics for each of the three regiments under his command.

He also knew the birth signs of each of his subordinate regimental commanders, so if Naylor decided that Scorpios, among whom my late Colonel was numbered, should avoid outdoor activity, all outdoor training for the regiment would be suspended until Naylor detected a more propitious juxtaposition of the stars. At the same time another commander, whose sign gave warning of the need for particular vigilance against someone who was not a friend, would be ordered to stand to at dawn for the next seven days against the probability of a German landing in his area.

As far as my own duties were concerned, it appeared that an even higher authority had ordered, as an experiment, the use of a reconnaissance unit equipped with an elementary type of armoured car which was to be used as a part of a flying column ferreting out information about enemy movements which not even the powers of R. H. Naylor could divine. To this end each regiment had been requested to supply ten of their most highly regarded other ranks to man the cars under my command. These other ranks, the Brigade Major informed me, were due to arrive the next day, with the cars following in the near future.

Over the next week or so my men arrived in dribs and drabs. And with each new arrival my spirits sank deeper and deeper into my boots. If these were the élite of the regiments, I thought, we might as well throw in the sponge there and then. It was obvious that this exercise was being used as a heaven-sent opportunity for each regiment to disembarrass itself of its least-wanted rank and file. My suspicions were confirmed with a vengeance when the last to arrive was the contingent from my own regiment. Out of the window of my office I saw the truck draw up in front of their billets. Last out after the tailboard had been let down was the shambling figure of none other than Private Bolton.

Documentation arrived later, and from a preliminary examination of their crime sheets it was evident that what I ought to be running was a reformatory, not the eyes and ears of the brigade, a dashing band of Scarlet Pimpernels which I had been given the honour to lead to glory.

Determined as usual to do my best, however, I called my entire force together and gave them a pep talk. When I came to the bit about being the eyes and ears of the brigade and explained that our task was to seek out the enemy and help to encompass his destruction, of course Private Bolton's hand was the first to shoot up in the air.

'You mean we go swimming out into the sea in those tank things and see if them Germans are coming our way. Right?'

'Don't be absurd, Bolton,' I snapped. 'We only come into action when they have landed.'

Then Private Roberts, another trouble-maker if ever I saw one, piped up. 'An' lying quiet as mice, not firin' their guns or anything so we got to go and find them. Sort of hide and seek.'

'That will be quite enough of that,' I said, feeling rather like a prim geography mistress not used to being baited at school.

Since there was no sign of our reconnaissance cars we fell victim to another of the Brigadier's obsessions: barbed wire, the efficacy of which to keep back the Hun he had no doubts whatsoever. His rock-solid faith in the stuff dated back to what he had been told about its efficiency in the First World War, although I doubt if he had had much practical experience at the time.

That the Germans had swept across Europe in 1940, ignoring such masterpieces of modern technology as the Maginot Line, did nothing to undermine his confidence in barbed wire—a confidence which appeared to be shared by the highest echelons of command. There might be difficulties in getting supplies of such military bric-à-brac as bullets, but at the snap of a finger barbed wire would arrive by the lorry load.

The barbed wire was made up in springy coils and the theory was that you laid two lengths of serpentine coils alongside each other, placed a third one on top and you had instantly produced an impregnable barrier, behind which you could move about in perfect safety while on the other side the enemy gnashed their teeth in frustration.

The Brigadier ordered that my 'élite corps' should be put to work surrounding Brigade HQ with these beastly treble coils of wire, which meant a lot of incredibly boring and hard work. Whole woods had to be cleared of impassable undergrowth (a far more effective deterrent than wire) and even large trees cut down in order to get the wire in position.

One night in the mess, after a rather better than usual dinner, I decided to tackle the Brigadier over the insanity of the whole concept.

'Surely,' I argued, 'when the Germans come up against this insurmountable barrier they will simply bypass it rather like the Maginot Line and leave as until we are starved out?'

'In that case, we shall die like gentlemen,' he declared. Then, wagging his finger at me, added: 'Have you forgotten Khartoum and Mafeking. They were both relieved, just as we shall be relieved.'

I determined to have one more try.

'Do you know, Sir, that it is in fact very easy to get through wire?'

'Impossible,' he declared, but nevertheless I managed to persuade him to come and watch a demonstration the next day.

The method is quite simple. One, preferably large, body

races up to the wire and does a belly-flop across it, which immediately squashes it down sufficiently for those behind to pour through, taking care to place their foot in the small of the recumbent soldier's back, rather like a form of leap-frog.

The Brigadier watched in silence. Then he said, 'The Germans will never think of that. It must be regarded as top secret information. They must never know.'

With that he walked away, clearly shaken. Shortly afterwards we were taken off wire and put on making camouflage nets for gun emplacements.

Then, thankfully, our armoured vehicles arrived. There were seven in all, each consisting simply of a large, square, cast-iron box on the chassis of a 3-ton truck. The driver's vision was restricted to a narrow slit, just like in a real tank, and the commander stuck his head through a square hole in the top, which also served as an exit and entrance for the rest of the crew. Crude they may have been but to my motley gang they were heaven-sent. Gone in a trice were the deadly chores of the wire and the camouflage nets. Instead, each morning, urged on

by the Brigadier, we would disappear into the surrounding countryside, equipped with haversack rations, select a suitable pub for a midday break, and return around suppertime as happy as schoolboys.

'How is the training going, Sutherland?' the Brigadier would ask every evening.

'Splendidly, Sir,' I would reply with confidence.

He never thought to ask for details as to the nature of this 'training', and indeed I would have been hard put for an answer. The fact is, one cannot concentrate on map-reading all day and every day. Instead we lent a hand with the harvest and were rewarded by friendly farmers with copious quantities of beer. Or we played football against teams largely made up of coal miners who had been given time off for Home Guard training. At other times, whenever any of the regiments to which we had recently belonged were engaged in some particularly arduous form of foot-slogging, we would take the greatest pleasure in tearing around in clouds of dust. 'Showing the flag' we called it.

All this activity had an amazing effect on the morale of my band of hitherto degenerate soldiery. The crime rate dropped to nil. Soon Bolton took to polishing the toe caps of his boots and the billets reached such a standard of orderliness that the Brigade Major took the opportunity of showing them off to officers visiting HQ.

Then came the TEWT, which stood for Tactical Exercise *with* Troops—unless of course it was of the indoor variety with sand tables and blackboards, which was also known as a TEWT, only this time it stood for Tactical Exercise *without* Troops. These exercises were held from time to time largely so that the more senior officers could try their hand at moving their units around in simulated conflict. They were held at all levels: company versus company, regiment versus regiment, brigade versus brigade, and so on. On more than one occasion most elaborate operations were held, involving practically every soldier in the country.

This particular exercise involved one division in Scotland supposedly attacking one division in England—which happened to be ours. The Brigadier went mad with excitement. He took to carrying the *News of the World* around with him wherever he went and, as the week when the exercise was due to begin approached, awaited the coming Sunday's edition with an impatience which was most painful to observe.

Of the three brigades which made up our division, ours was the only one with a reconnaissance unit, which made the Brigadier burst with pride. As a gesture of oneupmanship I was produced at conferences held at the highest level, where my three pips seemed dreadfully out of place surrounded by red tabs, crossed swords and crowns. Generously the Brigadier placed my services at the disposal of whichever brigade should be considered to need me most. I was to probe deep into enemy territory and not a sparrow must fall but it be reported back instantly. A fleet of motor cycles was put at my disposal to provide rapid communication with the appropriate brigade. There was even talk of wireless but it proved in the end to be too technical a matter. We were still living in the age of semaphore.

To overcome the difficulty of knowing who was winning or losing without the use of live communication, a huge band of umpires was appointed, to be recognized by a white band worn on one arm. When opposing forces came into confrontation there would be a crackle of blank cartridges and the umpires would dart around tapping people on the shoulders and saying 'You're dead'. The 'dead' soldiers were then required to fall over and lie still, which most people were quite glad to do, until that particular skirmish was over.

The umpire's decision, as in a game of cricket, was law, although there were to be regrettable incidents when umpire fell out with umpire and one would wipe out a whole platoon at a stroke in revenge for an imaginary wrong decision by another. It was all, as someone once said about sex, the best fun you could have without laughing.

This particular exercise was scheduled to last from Monday to Friday—we had not yet got into the bad habit of behaving in a warlike manner over the weekend. The Brigadier was in agony. His personal sign of the zodiac had warned him against making hasty decisions in the coming week and to avoid unnecessary travel.

'You must give me the earliest possible information about the enemy. To be forced to move my headquarters in a hurry could only be disastrous,' he implored me.

My lot, on the other hand, were cock-a-hoop. I realized that my strange-looking iron boxes as yet bore no distinguishing signs indicating to what unit or formation they belonged. Since there were seven of them I had only got so far as naming them after Sneezy, Dopey, Grumpy and the rest of the Seven Dwarfs. My own little car was Snow White.

My plan was to pack as many rations as we could scrounge into the Seven Dwarfs and swan off into the blue, harbouring for the night in any of the delightful little Northumberland villages which took our fancy, selected for the pulchritude of the local talent and the availability of beer supplies, rather than for military tactical advantage.

Thus on the first night we found ourselves deep behind the enemy lines, which were being moved forward at such a cautious rate that I doubted if our opponents would disturb the Brigadier before the weekend put a stop to further activity. I telephoned the Brigadier accordingly. 'Tortoise,' I told him in our cunningly rehearsed code. He was delighted. If I had said 'Hare' he would have spent a sleepless night.

Snugly ensconced in our chosen place of liquid refreshment, I was chatting to one of the unsuspecting enemy.

'Who are you lot then?' he asked.

'Divisional Headquarters troops,' I replied without much thought.

'Oh, just up the road then.'

'Who?'

'Div. HQ o' course.'

That was when the idea was first sown as a tiny seed. A couple more Newcastle Browns with Dodson, whom I had recently rather grandly promoted to the rank of Platoon Sergeant, Corporal Jason-Smith and Private Edgar, who was my batman/driver, and the idea blossomed in all its glory.

I must say the plan owed much of its brilliance to my OCTU training, which had laid down certain guidelines, if not dogmas, designed to mould a successful leader of men. At all times an officer must show initiative, display coolness and daring in the face of the enemy, and by his enthusiasm infuse the same spirit in his troops. He must be resourceful and, failing specific orders from higher authority, capable of making on-the-spot decisions.

If ever an opportunity offered itself to demonstrate these qualities, it was now. Here I was, in the heart of enemy territory and at the head of my intrepid, highly-trained unit. The invaders from the north, with whom we now found ourself sharing the same public bar, represented the Germans. So far we had escaped detection and, in fact, had won the enemy's confidence. Although Higher Command was still thinking defensively, now surely was the time to strike a body-blow which might well alter the whole course of battle? It was a situation in which VCs should surely be won. (When I was eventually faced with the real thing I found that my ambition to win the VC had evaporated. In times of danger it was the WC for which I felt the greater need.)

Nonchalantly I leant across the table and cupping my hand in front of my mouth said: 'Tonight, Dodson, we will take an important prisoner.'

John Dodson looked as though he thought the Newcastle Brown was proving a bit much for me. Suddenly his eyes brightened and a broad grin spread across his craggy features.

'Cor!' he said. Dodson always said 'Cor!', when he thought he'd grasped the idea.

'Cor! You mean we'll smuggle Blondie there back to the bivvy.'

We'd all been eyeing the luscious piece of goods who found it necessary to stand back some distance from the beer pumps, so outstanding were her more obvious charms.

I adopted my narrow-eyed look.

'Tonight,' I said, 'the reconnaissance platoon will capture the Divisional Commander of the invading force.'

There was a stunned silence.

'Fuck,' said Private Edgar.

Then Jason-Smith, who had been educated at Eton, exclaimed, 'I say, Sir, what an absolutely spiffing idea! Oh what a wheeze!'

I might add that he had been twice returned from OCTU as unsuitable officer material, which is presumably how he came to be in my lot.

I could see it was time to demonstrate my powers of leadership. I looked at my watch, and in my best incisive officer's manner, hissed out the following orders:

'Right, it is now approaching 2100 hours. You, Sergeant, will return to the laager area (I liked to use such real 'tankie' expressions when I could). You will be accompanied by Corporal Jason-Smith. Alert the task force. Four up under your command. Three in reserve under Corporal Jason-Smith. Ready to move off approx. 2200 hours. Private Edgar will stay here with me to collect vital information about the exact position of the objective. Understood?'

Jason-Smith, I thought, was about to leap to attention and salute. I could see even Dodson was pretty impressed. They slid out of the bar with all the furtive ostentation of pantomime villains.

I played it cool and boxed clever. Not for the first time I thought I'd make a fine agent behind enemy lines.

On the pretext of ordering another brown ale I stepped up to the bar where a couple of sergeants in the Signals were chatting.

'My damn fool driver has left my map behind,' I said, putting on my most languid officer's voice. 'Can you by any chance direct me to Div. HQ. Got to report to the G2 before turning in.'

'Turn right out of the door. Second left two miles, first right and you can't miss it. Red caps freezing their balls off outside the front gates. Sort of big country house place. Top brass do themselves all right, I'd say. Well, thank you, Sir, it's a couple of Guinness.'

The sergeant hardly bothered to look up. I didn't like to ask if he knew the password.

From that moment on the whole operation took on a sort of dream-like quality. Back at the laager I found the whole platoon already mounted, engines ticking over.

The plan was the essence of simplicity. I would go ahead in Snow White. Dodson's four tanks would be five minutes behind, then follow me up the drive while Jason-Smith in reserve would turn his vehicles, on the pretext of taking up guard position, but in reality in order to cover what I anticipated would be a fast getaway.

As a last-minute inspiration we all pulled Balaclava helmets well down over our faces so that only our eyes showed. It did much, I felt, to heighten the drama.

Just as the sergeant had said, there was no difficulty in locating HQ. And indeed red caps (military police) were stamping up and down outside the lodge gates. As Edgar made to turn in at the gates one of them held up his hand.

'Where do you think you're going?' he enquired, poking his head in at the window.

'Can't you see there's an officer in the car?' snapped Edgar with great presence of mind.

When it comes to bullshit there is no more disciplined body of men than the CMP. He snapped to attention and saluted in the darkness.

Whilst he examined the vehicle by the light of his torch, I got out slowly, pulled off my Balaclava and made sure that he could see my three pips.

'The HQ Armoured Guard are about to arrive,' I said with quiet authority. 'Only four vehicles are to enter the grounds. The remaining three will stay here. Only *four* inside, is that quite clear?'

'Perfectly clear, Sir,' said the red cap, looking hard at the car and saluting about four more times. 'Only four inside, Sir.'

Giving orders, I had quickly learned, was far easier than answering questions.

Shortly afterwards Dodson's iron boxes drew up behind me in the avenue under the trees.

'Right, Dodson. One man from each crew to follow me on foot. Turn vehicles and be ready to move as soon as we appear with the prisoner.'

The house was rather grand with a porticoed entrance at the top of an impressive spread of stone steps. One of my team, I noticed with some misgivings, was Private Bolton.

Signalling to my men to conceal themselves on either side of the doorway, I mounted the steps and rang the bell. It was answered almost immediately by a mess orderly in a white jacket.

'I have urgent dispatches for the General.'

The orderly held out his hand.

'To be delivered personally,' I snapped.

'He is upstairs in the billiards room,' said the orderly uncertainly.

82

'Edgar, cover this man! The rest follow me.' Bulldog Drummond in his finest hour could have done no better.

A moment later I was racing upstairs with four determined men at my heels. Conveniently, one room had 'Billiards Room' painted in yellowing letters on the door. I threw it open.

For a second or two the scene was a perfect *tableau vivant*. Two junior staff officers, engaged in a desultory game of snooker, stood open-mouthed, their cues poised in mid-stroke. At the far end, beside a roaring wood fire, four senior officers seated round a bridge table froze into immobility. Then, as one, they hit the floor—all that is except the General himself, resplendent in red tabs and glittering insignia. For a moment he stared at us curiously, then, quietly folding his cards, placed them neatly on the table.

'Ah,' he said simply.

From that moment, as the Newcastle Brown drained swiftly from my bloodstream and reality flooded back, the brave figure I imagined I was cutting rather shrivelled. Yet with only the slightest hesitation, I started a speech I had run over in my mind.

'You are my prisoner. Under the Geneva Convention you are only required to give me your name, rank and army number.'

'An' I've got me tommy-gun trained on yer belly-button,' added Bolton, but even that brave effort somehow lacked conviction.

Rather shame-faced, the other officers started to raise their heads over the edge of the billiards table and clamber to their feet. A colonel with a well-brushed moustache had, I noticed with some satisfaction, acquired a nasty cut on his forehead, presumably in his efforts to be first under the table.

It was the General himself who came to the rescue. He looked at me with what I thought might almost be indulgence.

'Very good,' he said. 'Very good indeed.' He turned to

another senior officer, who was gingerly dusting off his mess kit. 'Umpire,' he said. 'What is the position now in your view?'

'Well, if this officer has made adequate arrangements to escape back to his own lines I suppose I should have to declare you a prisoner of war.'

'Ah,' said the General again. I must say he was most interested. He even came down and had a look at the tin boxes. The guards were asked how we had got by without the password.

'Had it painted on 'is car 'e did,' said the CMP.

The password for that night, believe it or not, was Snow White.

'Fall out your men,' ordered the General. 'Care to join us in the mess for a nightcap?'

I accepted with alacrity. Things had not turned out too badly after all; he even asked me to take the Colonel's hand at the bridge table. The Colonel had a nasty headache.

The General and I won a seven hundred rubber. At least it paid for the Guinnesses.

'Right military fuck-up you made of that one, didn't you?' remarked Bolton when I rejoined my troop an hour later.

It was the last anyone heard of the matter.

Shortly after this heroic escapade I received an exciting letter from my Uncle Douglas who, in the opinion of all the rest of the family, was certifiable. Nevertheless, in the 1914–18 war he had won no less than six decorations for gallantry, including two DSOs. Father always maintained that he would never have won anything if he hadn't been as thick as two planks and the Germans such rotten shots. After that war he wandered off to the colonies prospecting for gold and finished up helping to run the Canadian Mounties.

Personally, I thought he was the greatest. Once, on one of his very rare visits home when I was around six years old, I was driving with him over a Highland road. Cars were still quite a novelty in my young life and I thought to ask him the purpose of the driver's mirror.

'So that you can keep an eye on anyone in the back seat who might try to stab you from behind,' he told me solemnly. Such was my faith in him that for many years I believed this unwaveringly.

In 1939 he had managed to get some mysterious job with the British Army and had written to say that he had made special application to the War Office that I should join him and that they would inform me of the details. Shortly afterwards the Brigadier got a message requesting my release for special duties, which involved a small matter of parachuting into Albania.

The Brigadier got into a fearful tizzy; R. H. Naylor was consulted, but he was not optimistic. Under my sign of the zodiac there was dark talk of bereavement (always a fair bet in time of war) and advice (as usual) about not making hasty decisions.

In the event there was not a great deal of decision-making to do. With the War Office letter came an instruction to report to the parachute training school at Tidworth in seven days' time. Three days later the order was countermanded. Much later I learned that Uncle Douglas was dead.

At the time I experienced a mixture of relief and disappointment. Certainly my first reaction at the idea of falling out of an aeroplane and relying on an expanse of knicker-silk to see me safely to the ground did not have any immediate appeal. On the other hand the prospect of spending much more of the war keeping Private Bolton and his mates amused was becoming a rapidly increasing depressant.

Then matters took a sudden turn of their own and, at a stroke, R. H. Naylor lost much of his say in the direction of military policy. The Brigade was to be disbanded and the Brigadier himself given well-earned retirement. While detailed orders were given for the disposal, change of role or conversion of the three regiments under his command, I was flattered to find a special instruction for my own small unit. We were to entrain at Newcastle Central station for an unknown destination. A carriage would be reserved for us and I would be given sealed orders which were on no account to be opened until we had started on our journey.

Any disappointment I may have felt over the Albanian affair was immediately swept away. Here was the very stuff of high drama.

CHAPTER 8

The very old train clanked huffily out of Newcastle station and headed north. But after a few miles it changed its mind and backed all the way to Newcastle. Then it took a deep breath and set out over the Tyne Bridge.

My contingent was accommodated in a reserved third-class carriage marked 'Military Only'. I alone had a first-class warrant and rather reluctantly took a seat in a carriage occupied solely by one red-faced, tweed-suited elderly gentleman with two cocker spaniels on the seat beside him. The secret orders were burning a hole in my pocket and I had the melodramatic urge to lock myself in the WC before opening them. Then I thought: even if I tear them up and flush them down the pan they might be picked up on the track and pieced together by an enemy agent. However, I realized I was in danger of loosing my grip on reality in the excitement of the occasion. So I casually rose from my seat, stepped out into the corridor and, while appearing to be engrossed in the passing countryside, ripped open the envelope.

The instructions read: 'Top Secret. Destroy after reading. To Captain D. Sutherland. Detrain troops Penrith station—ETA 1600 hours—Transport provided to final destination.'

I was a trifle disappointed. Penrith was, as I knew, a pleasant little township a few miles south of Carlisle. An aunt of mine had once lived close by. Yet despite the sense of anticlimax I tore the message into tiny pieces and over the next four or five miles fed the fragments out of the window.

While the guns thundered in the Libyan desert to announce the assault on Tobruk, little did I guess that I was about to become involved in one of the most secret operations of the whole war.

It was already dusk when our 3-ton truck drove through the impressively ornate gates of one of England's most stately homes. A mile or so further down the seemingly endless drive we pulled up at what, in the gathering gloom, appeared to be a hutted camp.

'You dismount here, Sir,' said the driver, who was wearing a black beret with a Lancer cap badge. As I clambered out of the cab a tubby figure appeared out of the darkness. There was something vaguely familiar about his stamping of feet and saluting.

'Is it yourself, Sorr?'

'Good God. Kelly! What the hell are you doing here? What on earth is that thing you have on your head?' He, too, was sporting a black beret. It looked like a pea on a turnip. I must say I was glad to see him.

'What's this all about?'

'Shh, Sorr! Me lips is sealed 'til you've sworn on the Holy Book. Me orders is to take you to the officers' mess.' Then, casting a glance at my unit being assembled out of the back of the 3-tonner, he added, 'There'll be a hot meal for your lot.'

We sloshed through the mud to a long building where I could hear a sound which always pleases and comforts me: a river gurgling nearby. Kelly left me at the door. 'Glad you've come, Sorr,' he said, and this time he gave me a warm handshake.

Inside all was warmth and light. An orderly appeared to take my greatcoat and indicated the ante-room. On entering, the first person I saw, warming his backside in front of a roaring fire and siphoning a sherry through his walrus moustache, was none other than my old CO Joe Soap.

'Ah, Sutherland,' he remarked, 'splendid. At least we now have a decent bridge four.'

Sergeant-Major Kelly had spoken no more than the truth. In the mess that night I encountered several of my old mates from the days when we had so bravely guarded the beaches of South Shields. Bereft of their King's Regiment badges they now bore the clenched fist insignia of the Royal Armoured Corps. Others in rather more dashing mess kit displayed a variety of regimental favours, indicating that they owed loyalty to divers Hussar or Lancer regiments. One, a Queen's Bay, had been at school with me, but like all the rest he would not explain what I might discover on the morrow. Altogether it was weird and frustrating.

'Don't worry,' said Mike Greenwood, who was also one of the company, when I asked where all the 'donkey wallopers'—the infantryman's term for the cavalry—came from. 'Nothing to do with horses.' I was reassured. Whenever I get on a horse I am apt to fall off the other side.

'Tanks,' he said, adding mysteriously 'of a sort.'

If anything that was worse. My total knowledge of the internal combustion engine could be written on the back of a postage stamp.

The next day I discovered, much to my disappointment, that my squad was not to be kept together as a unit. We were to be used to bring up to strength the three squadrons which made up the regiment. At a single stroke they had been transformed from privates in an infantry company to troopers in an armoured squadron, from truck drivers to tank drivers, from signalmen to wireless operators, from riflemen to gunners.

However, before any of this could happen, we all had to swear, as Kelly had said, on the Good Book.

I was sworn in by Joe Soap himself, utilizing a tattered old

Bible with many pages obviously missing. It must have been the only copy available.

'If you have any doubts at all about this,' he said, 'now is the time to say so. It will not be held against you if you back out.'

Well, I thought to myself, if some of the characters I know are in this it is no time to chicken out. I duly took the oath.

'I swear by Almighty God that I will not divulge any information helpful to the enemies of His Majesty's Britannic Government in the matter of the top secret operations in which of my own free will I am now about to be involved.'

Then I set off, as instructed, to swear in my squad.

I believe most of them thought I already knew the deadly secret and, as Kelly marched them in one by one, with a touching faith they took the oath without any hesitation. Of course, there were one or two predictable exceptions. Edgson wanted to know if the oath was binding, if he was later to convert to the Jewish faith—a step, he explained, Bolton and he were seriously considering. Taken off my guard I asked him why.

'Get all them Jewish holidays, Yom Kipper, Day of Atonement and all that lot. No C of E church parades. Stands to reason, don't it?'

'Fall out!' roared Kelly. 'Come back when you've had yer foreskin cut off. Hope they don't throw away the wrong part.' Edgson sighed and took the oath.

Bolton proved more practical. He wanted to know what the penalty was if he let the cat out of the bag. 'Dishonourable discharge?' he asked hopefully.

'As far as you're concerned, Bolton, they'll make an exception,' answered Kelly, speaking slowly and clearly. 'In your case they cut your balls off before they hangs you. By the Holy Mary they will.'

When the last man had been sworn in and Kelly and I were

alone, I asked him what it was all about. He took off his beret and scratched his head.

The parkland surrounding Lowther Castle, the family seat of the Earls of Lonsdale, in which we now found ourselves, was indisputably the largest in the country. The 5th Earl, himself one of the richest and most colourful characters over the past half century, had by that time retired to his hunting box in Leicester. Beloved by the sporting public—a sentiment not shared by his fellow aristocrats—he had spent most of his life in ostentatious display, which had included extending his park to enclose some 10,000 acres, most of it surrounded by an impressive stone wall. It was inside this great area that our secret operations were to be conducted.

To double the security the whole periphery of the park had been reinforced by miles of rather flimsy sackcloth which flapped in the wind and under or through which, it occurred to me, any inquisitive viewer might peer with the greatest of ease. This particular precaution became obviously more ludicrous when, a week or two after our solemn oath-taking, all was revealed to us.

We had inadvertently joined a part of our armoured forces referred to, neither unkindly nor inaccurately, as 'funnies'.

Instead of the conventional role of the Royal Armoured Corps in battle, great ingenuity was being shown in adopting armoured vehicles to all manner of other uses. For instance, there were the flails—tanks fitted with a length of whirling chain which thrashed the ground in front of them, designed to advance through minefields, explode mines and clear a path for the infantry. There were the amphibious DUKWs (appropriately known as ducks) which could cross rivers and many of which swam ashore at Arromanches on D-Day. And there were the flame-throwers which advanced like fire-breathing dragons, spewing forth great gobs of highly flammable napalm.

Besides these ferocious creatures our own speciality seemed at first sight tame indeed. Our offensive weapon was, to put it at its most simple, a rather powerful light. However, because at that time we did not have any actual tanks our indoctrination into this new type of warfare took the form of a series of lectures. The Army had just discovered moving pictures as an instructional aid and we were treated to endless film shows chiefly designed to impress upon us how much safer it was to go to war in a tank than on our flat feet. As 'commercials' they were not a great success, as a typical example will demonstrate.

'As you advance in your vehicle against the enemy,' a commentator would say in a brisk and cheerful voice, rather as if he was advocating the charms of a holiday camp, 'you may hear the enemy's fire tinkle against your heavily armoured hull. There is of course no need to feel alarm.' Minutes later the commentator would be extolling the lethal effects of our own armaments. An enemy tank would appear on the screen. 'Enemy vehicle approaching eleven o'clock left, fifteen hundred yards. Fire!' would come the crisp voice of the tank commander, and a German Tiger tank would be seen to disintegrate in a cloud of smoke.

'Tinkle, tinkle,' came a voice from the darkness.

'Trooper Bolton! Squadron Commander's orders tomorrow morning!' Sergeant-Major Kelly roared from the front row.

Boredom was once again setting in. Someone once remarked that war was one long bore interrupted by occasional screams of stark terror. We weren't even getting the odd minor shock.

In the days, now long past, when we had been snowbound on the Yorkshire moors, the songs of a talented, if bolshie, soldier called Melloy, sung on every occasion from route marches to canteen concerts, had done much to amuse and divert. Now, as we waited for something to happen, they reappeared in the troops' repertoire, along with 'Lili Marlene', 'Wish me luck as you wave me Goodbye', and other favourites. One of Melloy's songs started:

> Browned off, browned off,
> Browned off as can be.
> Browned off, browned off,
> An easy mark that's me.
> But when this war is over
> And again I'm free,
> They can go to bloody hell
> To save democracee——

Just as we were in imminent danger of reverting to the 'browned off' phase, with its usual consequences of minor crime, overindulgence in strong alcohol and general scruffiness all round, out of the blue our tanks arrived. The effect was dramatic. To have what we were assured was the most secret weapon of the war dropped into our laps was, to say the least, exhilarating. What we did not know until much later was that this particular device had been invented by a Greek and installed in a secret dungeon in the depths of Lowther Castle itself.

Basically they were Churchill tanks, on which the gun turret had been replaced by a specially constructed, heavily armoured housing for an immensely powerful light generated by the fusion of a positive and negative carbon rod. This light threw a beam against a highly polished concave mirror angled to project the beam back, magnified to something like two million candlepower, through a narrow slot in the turret hull. The slot was fitted with a shutter and when the shutter was opened a brilliant shaft of light illuminated the darkness with such startling clarity as to be blinding to anyone within its range of well over a thousand yards.

Not only did the beam immediately make the enemy seen

without being able to see, but the shutter could be operated to open and close with great rapidity, which had a dazzling and dazing effect so that it was impossible for the enemy to aim their weapons even in the rough direction of the opposition. Nor was it possible to gauge whether the lights were stationary or moving forward. Add to this the ability to switch the white light through most of colours of the rainbow, combined with a powerful voice booming through a loud-speaker and giving dire warning of a permanent loss of eyesight, and it will be readily understood that the whole contraption had distinct possibilities as an offensive weapon.

The real beauty of the CDL tank was, however, the tactical use to which it could be put. (CDL stood for Canal Defence Light, a name dreamed up by someone with an astonishingly high IQ, and cunningly designed to mislead anyone of even marginally lower intelligence.) The tanks were designed to be used in combinations of three or more, set in line about 50 yards apart and controlled by wireless from a command tank. On the command 'Open the gate. Now!', the combined beams from each tank, in theory at least, illuminated an 'objective' with their stark, hard light, the beam from each tank intersecting with its neighbour's at a distance predetermined by the distance between the tanks. This in turn created 'cloaks of darkness' in which infantry could move forward well ahead of the tanks and thus arrive on top of the enemy positions without any danger of being shot at.

Although, as I have already mentioned, I have no mechanical bent—let alone any skill as a lighting engineer—I entered into this game with our new toy with unbounded enthusiasm. So did everybody else, from Trooper Bolton upwards. It was like reliving the heady days of our reconnaissance platoon all over again, only with a clearer purpose. In another part of the global conflict in which we were all involved Jerry was being chased out of Africa. A German invasion of Britain seemed unlikely and, indeed, there were many who were forecasting that the time was not far distant when we should be crossing the Channel in the opposite direction. And lighting, literally, the path to ultimate victory would be none other than the brigade of which our regiment was a proud member.

Obsessed as everyone was with the extreme secrecy of the operation, we were put to learn a set of codewords by which our nocturnal operations were conducted. There was an unwavering conviction that the Germans had a team of expert decodifiers on a 24-hour listening watch, striving to crack the meaning of such commands given over a B set (range approximately 500 yards) as 'Open the gate', 'Scatter', and 'Moonlight'. Unit commanders were always referred to as 'Sunrays', their superiors 'Super Sunrays', and so on in order of rank until at the very highest echelons of military command one ran out of adequate superlatives.

At the height of our operations the electricity bills of the honest citizens of Penrith plummetted to near zero as they read their newspapers by the lights of our nightly manoeuvres on the Cumberland fells. Of course, the miles of ineffective sackcloth had long since blown away.

Our nightly exercises did not always run entirely smoothly. Having got one's tank into approximately the right position on the start line, and mindful of the ever-listening ears on the other side of the Channel, things would start off well enough.

'Prepare to open the gate.'

'Open the gate now!'

Then a distinct deterioration in security was apt to set in.

'Number three, what the fuck's happened to your light?'

'Me bleedin' carbon's busted.'

'Well put in a new one. There's a bloody great black hole on the objective.'

'Number three troop prepare to advance.'

'Advance now!'

'Number two, what the hell's keeping you?'

'Thrown a track. Take us half an hour to fix it.'

'All right, everybody. Close the gate. Fall out for a smoke and we'll try it again.'

When the rains came the whole of our training area, already pulverized to such an extent that scarcely a blade of grass survived, degenerated into a quagmire. To step off the hull of a bogged-down tank was to sink into a grey morass of mud. The smell of diesel and of burning mud thrown up against the tank exhausts became as pervasive in our lives as the scent of attar of roses in a French brothel, although hardly as sweet. We alternately sweated or froze—and stank all the time.

We became night birds for three nights and then had three nights off. Sundays were set aside for the worship of God or contemplation of our navels, according to individual tastes. There was a great deal of navel contemplation. One soldier caused a seven-day wonder by getting what was described as 'a self-inflicted wound', a euphemism for venereal disease. He was court-martialled, the only reason for this drastic action being, as far as I could gather, because it was contracted anally.

Buggery was not, however, as I understand to be frequently the case in an entirely male society living in close proximity, particularly prevalent. Indeed, accustomed as we were to turning night into day while on training, we continued to do so in our leisure time, descending on defenceless females in Penrith and other hospitable centres at nightfall, returning to camp in the early hours to sleep off our excesses in what might remain of the morning, until 'Come to the Cookhouse Door' was sounded around midday.

Afternoons were devoted to various forms of indoor or outdoor training, according to the weather. Joe Soap, possibly influenced by the fact that I had the modest reputation of being able to hit the odd driven pheasant, had appointed me Regimental Gunnery Officer. This necessitated not only organizing instruction on the use of every weapon, ranging from the grenade to revolvers, but having to master the intricacies of the Besa machine gun with which our tanks were equipped. This was made maddeningly difficult by the Army's insistence that every man should learn the correct description for each component part, presumably so that if something broke or went missing he could personally indent for a replacement from Ordnance. However, since the smallest and easiest-to-lose part of the Besa was a vital but minute split-pin described in the manual as 'pin retaining nut retaining body-locking shaft', it will be understood that my task was a fairly uphill one. All I could really hope for was that when it came to the crunch the tank gunner would know where the bloody trigger was.

Incidentally, the official manual for the use of the Quartermaster indenting for supplies held its occasional rewards, such as one item which read, 'Pots, rubber, officers, lunatic, for the use of'.

Our routine was punctuated at intervals by visits from higher authority. Such manifestations were not altogether unwelcome since they held both advantages and disadvantages. That a visit from a VIP was imminent was heralded by a sudden flurry of frenetic and tiresome activity at Brigade level. The Brigadier himself might even appear, but he was a sort of Greta Garbo figure who did not normally show at grassroots level. More often he sent his Brigade Major who had a habit of stalking round the billets or the tank park, lashing his riding boots with a leather swagger stick, and with Joe Soap and the Adjutant dancing attendance. He would then put in an appearance in the mess, knock back a couple of gin and tonics, give it as his considered opinion that Dante was the best two-year-old in training, and disappear again in a cloud of dust or mud. His visit would be followed by a tiresome period of barrack-room inspections and fatigue parties detailed to clear up any empty beer bottles or such other impedimenta as might be lying around.

The plus side of these visits was that they sparked off pleasurable speculation as to who the VIPs might be on that particular occasion. In the earliest days they were disappointingly small fry, sometimes a party of American brass hats, sometimes a flurry of generals, air marshals, and even admirals. We never knew who they were likely to be until we opened up with the CDL beams concentrated on a group of haystacks where the VIPs were wont to assemble.

Then, as news of the landings in Italy filtered through, we really moved into the big time. One 'Super-Super-Super-Sunray' night revealed the familiar figure of General Eisenhower surrounded by his aides. Another night which occasioned even more excitement was when General Montgomery was revealed in the glare of the footlights, with King George VI more modestly positioned to the great man's right rear. It was, however, predictable that when Winston Churchill himself appeared he should up-stage the rest of them put together. Oddly enough, his visit was not preceded by the usual spate of rumours and abnormal activity on our part. However, when his stocky figure was suddenly exposed to the glare of several million candlepower, 'even the ranks of Tuscany could scarce forbear to cheer', particularly when it was observed that while in his right hand the great man held the familiar cigar, his left hand was engaged with a similarly shaped, if more personal, object. Having completed the watering of the haystack at his leisure he calmly zipped up his famous boiler suit, clamped the cigar in his mouth and applied his complete attention to the entertainment for the evening.

As time went by it became increasingly obvious that it was our destiny to be the means of delivering the final dagger thrust at the heart of the enemy. If anybody had any doubts in this matter they were dispelled instantly when arrangements were suddenly announced for everyone to have home leave, the surest possible sign that tough times lay ahead. The Army had always considered it good for morale that all ranks should have an opportunity of saying goodbye to their loved ones.

That night in the mess I discussed this sudden turn of events with Peter, one of my closest friends. Should we return to share for a brief spell the rigours of civilian life with our families? Or,

instead, should we go up to London, stay in the best hotel we could find and devote ourselves to an orgy of eating, drinking and fornication, if possible in the reverse order of urgency? We carefully weighed the pros and cons, but, under the circumstances, there was nothing profound about the decision Peter and I came to regarding our unexpected leave.

One of the most frustrating aspects of the sort of war I had experienced up to that time was the knowledge that while we were playing boy scouts a lot of other people were getting killed or wounded. For instance we had just heard that Monte Cassino had finally been taken with appalling casualties. There must have been few of our age who could not count friends amongst the dead and wounded.

It was a subject which we always attempted to keep at a most dispassionate level. Someone reading a letter at breakfast might look up suddenly and say:

'By the way, did you know D. R. P. Gordon?'

'You mean "Bratter"? Yes, of course, I was at school with him.'

'Become dead; shot up at Tobruk.'

'Oh.'

There would be a short, awkward silence and then somebody else would say 'Pass the marmalade'.

It was only afterwards, perhaps when I had sneaked off to enjoy my passion for trout fishing and was rhythmically casting down a pool, that thoughts of the spotty boy who used to sit at the desk in front of me—the same boy I had delighted in tormenting with flicked pellets of soggy blotting paper—would intrude and I would find myself crying great sploshy tears. The odd thing about this was that had somebody told me that Bratter had been run over by a bus I would certainly have been sorry to hear of it but equally certainly I would not have become lachrymose. Were they then tears of anger rather than of sympathy? If so, anger against whom? Surely not the enemy, who were only trying to do to us what we were trying to do to them? I don't think many fighting soldiers were motivated by anger, although I must admit that I was to lose my temper from time to time in the heat of battle.

Neither of us had visited the beleaguered capital since the first year of hostilities, and almost immediately after booking in at the Savoy we wished we hadn't come. This owed nothing to the standard of elegance and near luxury which the Savoy Hotel had managed somehow to retain, but rather to the shock of seeing London battered to a skeleton of its pre-war affluent image we so well remembered.

However, an hour or so luxuriating in hot water revived our spirits. After paying special attention to our badly neglected mess kit, we descended to the cocktail bar, there to fire the opening shots in our campaign to plumb the depths of debauchery.

The barman, Harry Craddock, who an age later I was to count amongst my closest allies and friends, raised an elegant eyebrow of enquiry.

'A dry Martini?', Peter suggested.

'*Very* dry, Sir?'

'Very,' said Peter. Peter had the odd knack of appearing to wear an old Etonian tie, despite the strict limitations of a cavalry officer's mess kit, which commanded for him immediate respect as a man of the world. An elderly poof at the other end of the bar in a brightly spotted Churchillian bow tie nodded approvingly. The bar started to fill up with countless Americans, several languid-looking uniformed war correspondents, and an Australian Air Force group captain with the ribbons of the DSO and DFC peeking out apologetically from under his lapel.

We were on our third dry Martini—the maximum ration, we were told by Harry—when there was the most frightful bang. For a moment the bar seemed to sway and glasses slid crazily down the counter. A few people sitting at small tables beat a quick retreat. Only the fact that nobody at the bar blinked an eye stopped Peter and I following suit.

'Blackfriars, I would have thought,' somebody remarked conversationally.

'Definitely City direction,' another agreed.

'Harry, do you think under the circumstances my ration might extend to a couple of Martinis for our two friends?' The poof nodded benignly in our direction. Harry shook them up without protest.

That was the first time we had heard a bomb explode in anger, and although we were to experience a few more loud bangs before we got back to the safety of Cumberland, that first one was humbling. Also, it was the first time we were given some idea of what courage was all about. Only it seemed very odd that we should have experienced it sitting in the cocktail bar at the Savoy Hotel.

Numerous accounts of the war pay tribute to the incredible spirit shown by those at the receiving end of German bombing raids, and in London this fortitude must surely have reached its apotheosis. The heroism of the civilian army of air-raid wardens, fire fighters, rescue teams and other auxiliaries was matched in equal measure by those with a stoical determination simply to endure.

As for Peter and I, insulated as we had been for so long against the realities of war, the shock was enormous and the mental adjustment not easy to make. The total impenetrable darkness of the streets after nightfall, punctuated by oases of brightly-lit bars behind whose heavily shuttered windows a sea of khaki-clad bodies strove to catch the eye of overworked bar attendants, was not at all the idyllic stroll through the pastures of pleasure we had planned for ourselves.

Had it not been for the lucky chance that we had hit on the Savoy as our headquarters, with the cocktail bar, as it were, the operations room, the whole exercise would have been doomed to failure. Harry's bar had all the elements of a good club, and the members who met there punctually each morning for an eye-opener were generous with advice on how and where we were best likely to enjoy ourselves under such adverse conditions. Introductions were arranged to such exclusive *boîtes de nuit* as the 400 and the Embassy, where by some mysterious process one could buy unlimited supplies of whisky—at a price—to be kept in store or replenished, as the case might be, against a future visit.

It was, surprisingly, our friend of the Churchillian bow tie, whom we had discovered was a writer of world acclaim, who first personally escorted us. On a night when the sky was aflame and the staccato bark of anti-aircraft fire was at its height, we made our way to a basement tucked in behind Regent Street. After the most careful screening we were admitted to a room where the décor, in addition to the normal alcoholic display, relied for its effect almost entirely of a bevy of very beautiful girls. Their contribution to the war effort, our benefactor explained gently, was to relieve the tensions of battle-fatigued gentlemen of high social standing. The screening at the door was not a precaution against intervention by the law, from whom the club appeared to have acquired complete immunity, but to ensure that the candidates for admission belonged to an acceptable regiment.

Several days and nights later, two very tired and battle-fatigued officers duly caught a train back to resume the peaceful prosecution of the war against their country's enemies.

CHAPTER 9

Back in camp we found ourselves at once plunged into frenetic activity. Another large-scale exercise was being planned, and although hitherto, presumably on account of the extreme secrecy of our operations, we had been excluded from these periodical affairs, now we were to show our paces against real troops rather than a restricted number of VIPs.

The history of this memorable exercise can be quickly told. Higher Command's fervent imagination had been working overtime. Instead of a situation in which the implacable forces of aggression ('the baddies') were represented as sweeping down from the north, to be repelled by 'the goodies' (us), this time it was the goodies whose role it was to attack the aggressors and win a famous victory.

Also, it was contrived that a battalion of a certain distinguished regiment should find itself, after an arduous day of rearguard fighting, dug in and determined to fight to the last man or commit the equivalent of hara-kiri. It was against this last, desperate and defiant stand that an hour after darkness fell we should play our trump card.

When the time arrived the determined defenders, who had indeed endured a day of hard tactical withdrawal as decreed by the umpires, were warned that their night might not go unmolested. Nevertheless, they were to stand their ground come what may and need have no fear that they were other than guinea-pigs in an experiment from which they would suffer no grievous harm.

On the command 'Open the gate!' everything went according to plan. Our support infantry, revelling in this new experience, advanced, concealed in their 'cloaks of darkness' and hugging themselves gleefully in anticipation of the moment when they would fall upon the enemy crying such pleasantries as 'Ya-boo you're dead. I've just stuck a bayonet up your arse!'

Alas, this pleasure was not to be. As the infantry swept over the carefully prepared defensive positions there was not a hair of the enemy to be seen. The slit trenches were deserted and only an assortment of arms, empty mess tins and discarded articles of clothing and equipment gave evidence of their recent occupation. It took until well after daybreak before the enemy were able to reassemble their scattered forces.

All of us, of course, were cock-a-hoop. If a pre-warned battalion of trained men could be so easily thrown into reverse gear, imagine the devastating effect on a real enemy!

We were to know the official response soon enough. Scarcely a week later a conference of all officers was called in the mess. When the Brigadier and the Brigade Major entered there was a ripple of anticipation. This was undoubtedly going to be it.

'Gentlemen,' said the Brigadier. 'I have to inform you that I have just returned from consultations at the very highest level. In fact,' he added, puffing himself up like a bullfrog, 'I was called into consultation with the Joint Chiefs of Staff. You will all be aware that the day when the Allied forces will invade Europe cannot be far off. As to the exact date my lips are sealed. However, I am able to give an official denial of certain rumours which have been spread among you and which have come to my ears. There is no immediate prospect that the Brigade under my command will be engaged in an operation which may be imminent, nor indeed in the longer term. With effect from this date, therefore, all further training will be suspended.'

He stood for a moment with a smug look on his face as if he expected a standing ovation.

Nobody moved. He turned abruptly and left in a silence broken only by the whack of the accompanying Brigade Major's swagger-stick beating a tattoo on his riding boots.

As the door closed behind them, the initial response came from an officer who had forgotten his temporary status as a gentleman.

'Fuck me,' he said.

This exhortation just about summed up the general feeling of all those present.

Rumours and counter-rumours circulated in whirlpools of conjecture and speculation. Most people blamed the Brigadier. 'Always said he was a windy bugger,' Trooper Bolton gave as his opinion. Be that as it may, the next thing we knew was that we were kissing goodbye to the mud and diesel fumes of Lowther Park. We left not as King Arthur's Knights in search of the Holy Grail, nor even as a collection of Don Quixotes ready to tilt at enemy windmills, but we stole away as thieves in the night, leaving the good citizens of Penrith to pay higher electricity bills in the future and, we hoped, to cherish some memories as happy as our own—destination Newmarket, prospects bleak.

(Later on, towards the end of the war, when I found myself serving on General Montgomery's staff at 21 Army Group, I was to hear that this eleventh-hour decision was a result of Eisenhower's insistence that if the British were to have CDL it should also be available to the Americans. Monty, on the other hand, wanted to keep it to himself. That such pettiness should result in neither of the Allies agreeing on a policy, albeit apparently to their mutual advantage, was by no means without precedent.)

Not surprisingly, once the umbilical cord had been severed the whole spirit of the battalion underwent a complete change. It seemed almost as if it shrugged, put its feet up and settled down to a contented if premature retirement. The invasion of Europe, once so eagerly discussed and looked forward to, was regarded as a matter of purely academic interest. There were, of course, some among our number in the officers' mess who continued to make warlike noises and generally expressed their frustration by getting hugely drunk whenever opportunity and adequate supplies of alcohol offered.

However, although two distinct factions had been created in the mess, there was still some suspicion that not all the boozers were necessarily militants, nor all those pacifically inclined of more moderate habits. The Colonel himself, while he continued to strain his normally modest intake of sherry through his moustache before dinner, was undoubtedly on the side of the militants. There had always been some doubt in many minds whether, in fact, on account of his age he would, in the end, lead us into battle, but there could be not the slightest doubt that to get into battle under any pretext was his highest ambition.

It was on the last day of April, 1944, that the Colonel announced his intention of going up to London, 'to see about things,' as he confided to the Adjutant, although just what these 'things' were was not at all clear.

The following morning he appeared at breakfast in the greatest of good humour. At the time I was under a considerable cloud in his books over the quality of the port I had been able to obtain in my capacity as President of the Mess Committee. To discover that overnight I had been restored to the favour of being addressed by my first name was as surprising as it was gratifying.

We had not long to wait to learn the reason for his high spirits. An officers' conference was called for mid-morning. When everyone was seated Joe Soap bounced in dead on cue

107

with the second-in-command (definite militant) looking like the cat who had got at the cream and the Adjutant (a suspect pacifist) looking like a bank clerk with a cash deficit.

The Colonel had been to the War Office. He had seen a very high-ranking officer indeed and created merry hell. He had failed to secure what he wanted, which was an assurance that the battalion under his command would have a definite role to play in the forthcoming offensive. However—and here Joe paused dramatically while his monocle fell out of his eye and was left to swing unheeded against his 1914–18 war medals—

'I have received an assurance at the very highest level that each and every member of this battalion from the highest rank to the lowest may immediately volunteer for service in a combatant unit of the Royal Armoured Corps and will, gentlemen I repeat *will*, have the opportunity of taking part in the first wave of the invasion of Europe, which we all know to be imminent.'

The silence which followed this triumphant announcement was almost as profound as that on an earlier occasion when the Brigadier had sounded the death knell of our aspirations to lead the British Army to final victory.

Then the Adjutant intoned gloomily, 'Squadron commanders will be responsible for ensuring that all ranks are informed. All applications to be in my office within 48 hours.'

Later, when the list of volunteers was revealed, it proved a trifle duller than might have been expected, amounting to a total of five officers and fourteen other ranks. As I read it over, I noted with a certain amount of pride that it included ten of my old reconnaissance platoon.

The following week I was at the saddling enclosure at Newmarket, watching the horses parade for the 2.30 on the first day of the May meeting, when somebody nudged me.

'How about a divvi till pay day?' whispered Trooper Bolton conspiratorially.

'What the hell for?' I asked. It had not been the first request of the sort in our long acquaintance.

'To put on that big black bugger.' He nodded towards the majestic Dante ambling round the ring.

I slipped him ten bob. 'Tell me, Bolton,' I said, 'are you out of your mind or something? I saw your name on the list. What are you doing volunteering? I thought it was against your principles.'

He favoured me with one of his lop-sided grins and said, 'You know me, Sir. I'll only get into trouble if I hangs around here much longer.'

'What's your posting?' I asked. I might have known it: we'd been posted to the same unit.

'Here,' he said, 'you done something naughty?'

He was looking at my epaulettes, now modestly adorned with the insignia of a lieutenant. Having once, with the support of R. H. Naylor, been one of the youngest captains in the Army, I had only recently been reflecting that my subsequent rate of progress threatened me with becoming one of the oldest. By volunteering for active service, however, even that which I had had been taken away. All volunteers were required to drop a rank, presumably on the grounds that they could be used to replace less senior casualties without offending the susceptibilities of seniority-conscious survivors.

'Like to see them make me drop a rank!' commented Trooper Bolton. Then he added, 'Do me a favour. Put a quid ante-post for me on that Dante for the Derby next year.'

He was about to wander off when I found myself saying, somewhat self-consciously, 'Bolton. Good Luck.'

'Do me a favour,' he replied. 'Turn it in.' And with a final 'Don't forget about that quid,' he gave me the thumbs-up sign and set off jauntily towards the Silver Ring. He looked, to use one of his own deplorable expressions, 'as happy as a pig in shit'.

It was the last I saw of him until shortly before D-Day.

The crossing, in the bowels of the tank landing craft, crammed head to tail like sardines on the tiered wire racks that passed for bunks, was not without its lighter moments.

I had waited until everyone had got themselves stowed away and, I hoped, stopped sicking up. Then Jim 'Jumbo' Botham, one of my closest buddies and my bridge partner during the whole of the Lowther Castle escapade, and I had tried to get up a game to pass the time. Understandably, there were no takers. A quiet game of cards was something the planners had made no arrangements for. As it was, just making one's way over piles of kit and prone bodies to the latrines (or 'heads' as they are oddly named in the navy) was a major effort.

So we decided, the uncomfortably cold wind notwithstanding, that we'd be better off on deck for a while. Leaning over the aft rail the darkness was so intense that we could scarcely make out the white spume behind the tank landing craft as it ploughed steadily through the increasingly choppy waters of the Channel. Occasionally a gust of wind blew a flurry of salt spray into our faces.

A figure appeared out of the darkness and leant on the rail by my side.

'Odd,' it remarked conversationally in an unmistakable public school accent, 'very odd how the middle classes are so easily afflicted by sea sickness.' It took me quite half a minute before I identified those well-modulated tones.

'Jason-Smith!'

'Now transformed, thanks to an obviously purblind commandant of yet another OCTU, into a higher social echelon. An officer *and* a gentleman no less.'

The last I had seen of him was just before our little unit had broken up in Northumberland and I had managed to obtain for him yet another shot at gaining a commission.

'Glad you made it.'

'I sometimes wonder. They were a lot of fun those days in the ranks. I got quite attached to my Geordie accent. In fact I had a job getting rid of it. Never do with my new lot.'

He was now, it transpired, a lieutenant in the Brigade of Guards.

'Flying high,' commented Jumbo, a trifle sourly I thought.

'I suppose it helps if you have an Earl for a cousin,' replied Jason-Smith in cheerful mockery.

We laughed, and suddenly the whole situation seemed incredibly funny, even the sound of yet another victim of *mal de mer* retching over the side.

'I suppose you got a copy of Monty's exhortation?' asked Jason-Smith.

We had. Indeed, it was an offence for any soldier to be making the momentous crossing of the Channel in June, 1944, in the general direction of France without having read, or having had read to him, the heroic (if unacknowledged) words of the Marquess of Montrose in Monty's pre-invasion script:

> He either fears his fate too much,
> Or his deserts are small,
> That puts it not unto the touch,
> To win or lose it all.

Brave words, I had always thought, from a man writing to his lover just when he was about to lose it all; but perhaps not entirely appropriate for Joe Bloggs on his way to liberate the Frogs and hopeful of getting safely away with it. Personally, I had never felt that it was awfully good form to advise troops, however poetically, of the imminent likelihood of their being reunited with their Maker, particularly on the eve of a frolic such as the one on which we were all now currently engaged.

I said as much to Jason-Smith, to whom it then occurred to

enquire after the health of our much appreciated Colonel Joe.

'Joe Soap,' I said reflectively. 'You know, he was a decent old stick whatever you lot thought. I think that he was terribly cut up that he was not going to get a chance in the end. Damn nearly blubbed when it came to saying good-bye. I heard he chucked his command next day.'

Jumbo nodded in the darkness. Actually, I didn't see him nod but he made the sort of burping noises which passed in his vocabulary for 'OK. Let's leave it in four spades.'

When I finally got myself stowed away on my wine rack it occurred to me vaguely that in a few short hours it was going to be the moment when the prompter in the wings would hiss 'you're on!'

Could there be any truth in Dr Johnson's assertion that the prospect of being hung concentrates the mind wonderfully?

I noted that in the bunk below me Jumbo was snoring happily. Before I could ponder the matter too deeply, I also fell soundly asleep.

CHAPTER 10

When I woke the engines were silent. For a moment I had the fantastic idea that I had overslept, that the war had rolled on and France had been liberated without my assistance.

Jumbo's bunk was empty but soon I heard the reassuring sounds of movement all around. Some men were struggling into various pieces of kit, previously discarded in the interests of comfort. Others were making their way up on deck, bumping into those on the way down, bearing, miraculously, steaming mugs of tea. There was quite a lot of barely polite cursing. Jumbo arrived and shoved a mug in my hand.

'Still pitch outside,' he reported. 'We're standing about half a mile offshore waiting our turn. Quite a bit of a snarl-up. Everybody banging into everybody else. First wave well dug in. No problems.'

As a situation report it was commendable for its brevity, if not exactly earning full marks for accuracy. Particularly the bit about no problems.

Everybody had been ordered to stand-to ready to land at around 4 am. Certainly it was bloody early and bloody cold. At such a time I almost found it in my heart to envy the British Tommy his Field Service Marching Order, a mode of dress and equipment laid down sometime around the turn of the century and adapted thereafter to more modern needs only by additions to the accoutrements. As well as the basic battledress, greatcoat and ammunition boots, there was the incredibly intricate canvas harness consisting, among other essential impedimenta, of webbing equipment, ammunition pouches, gas mask, haversack, waterbottle and blankets strapped on to a back pack—all this before coming to any form of armament, which might consist of anything from rifle and bayonet to an anti-tank rifle or 2-inch mortar. Even if all this gear rendered the wearer almost completely immobile, at least in moments such as these it provided some protection against the elements.

Tank crew members were allowed a little more latitude in matters sartorial. Personally, I was making the trip in a tank suit, with the addition, as an optional extra, of a nice fur-lined jacket given to me by a girlfriend, but which, on account of its length, could justifiably be described as a bum-freezer. Jumbo had sought refuge from the cold in something that looked suspiciously like a Harlequins rugger shirt.

Once on deck, Jumbo, Jason-Smith and I reappropriated our aft-rail stations of the night before. It immediately became evident that we were still rather more than half a mile from shore, the intense darkness somewhat relieved by the light of what looked like haystacks and houses burning in the distance.

It also became apparent by this distantly reflected light that we were by no means alone. Ploughing towards France, we had been so isolated by the darkness as to give the illusion that our small craft constituted the total reinforcement. Now, as dawn started to break, it was revealed that we were hemmed in on all sides by an enormous armada of vessels, some as small as modest cabin cruisers, others positive leviathans, their decks crowded to Bank Holiday proportions with khaki-clad figures.

I am sure that over the previous few weeks the odd attack of the colleywobbles, however privately, about how we would react when the moment of truth arrived had been experienced by most of us. I am also sure it is a truth rather than a truism that the worst fear is the fear of being afraid. Equally I am sure now that there had been no good and brave soldier in the history of arms who has not known fear and that the supreme act of bravery is in overcoming it.

Leaning against the rail on that bleak morning of 7 June, 1944, however, not one of us was in the least concerned that the moment of truth was upon us, and that in a few short minutes we might be called upon to 'put it to the touch, to win or lose it all'.

Instead, our eyes were riveted to the spectacle which had started to unfold bit by bit as dawn broke, like the lights going up in a theatre. All our thoughts and imaginings were centred on the magical *son et lumière* being enacted, as if for our special benefit.

It was only half light when the first bright flashes could be seen far out in the Channel, followed by the comforting swish of 16-inch shells passing high over our heads to land ten miles or more inland. Soon, on the skyline, we could see the dark silhouettes of the great warships and before long the landing beaches themselves came into focus. They were already crowded but there was such a crush of ships between us and the shore that it was obvious that there was little likelihood of being able to join them for some considerable time.

There were also quite a few nasty bangs.

Somebody said, 'Probably just mines going off. Not all cleared up yet.'

'I don't give a shit if they are mines going up or shells coming down. Much the same effect,' remarked somebody else and I could not but agree with him.

Time passed remarkably quickly and, with some surprise, I realized that it had already gone midday when our ship's engines started up again and we moved forward in an attempt to barge our way through the crush. We could see great activity among the infantry, cumbrously pushing up towards the sharp end, moving like so many heavily-armoured knights of old, but without their horses.

It must have been all of an hour later when, with a brave spurt, our landing craft finally beached itself and we started to pour ashore. We were among the lucky ones. Many in more unweildy craft had no alternative but to jump for it and get very wet indeed—or worse.

Our fellow passengers were mostly from one regiment (the Seaforth Highlanders, I believe) and somebody in command had formed them up and seemed to have some rough idea of the direction in which they were supposed to be heading. We other dribs and drabs, who had been included, one rather felt, as a sort of afterthought, had been told by the embarkation officer, 'Get ashore in one piece and ask your way to reinforcement HQ. They'll know where to find the units to which you have been allocated.' To which he added, 'I hope,' with what, with hindsight, I now know was considerable optimism.

It was very bewildering and I was forcibly reminded of a much-quoted remark made by a rather precious young officer who had survived the retreat from Dunkirk in 1940. Asked what it had been like he had commented with a languid wave of the hand, 'My *dears*. The *noise*; and the *people*!' As a description of our landing on Sword beach I could not have put it better.

There were a lot of people on stretchers waiting for a return passage—also a lot of people who would not be needing stretchers. The dead for the most part had been laid out in neat rows, as if still on parade. This was a practice which the British seemed to adopt even at the height of conflict, unlike the Germans who were apt to leave their dead all higgledy-piggledy. Worse, sometimes they wired them to booby-traps so that tidy-minded medical orderlies, surely among the bravest of all, were liable to get blown up for their trouble.

I suppose there was a good reason for this tidiness in

arranging the dead—perhaps it was the best way of ultimately facilitating the recovery of the bodies—but it had an odd effect on me. I found myself looking critically at their boots and gaiters, noting a broken lace here, some studs missing there. I imagine it stopped me from looking at their faces. They had ceased to be people and I did not want to know them, even if one or two had been personal friends of mine. It helped a lot to see them just as cardboard cut-outs at some charade.

Soldiers who were not dead or wounded were moving about everywhere. Some moved purposefully; others milled about with a sort of bewildered aimlessness which I subsequently came to recognize as a state of shell-shock.

Jumbo, Jason-Smith and I had decided to stick together, at least until we could find somebody who might have an inkling of where we were meant to be. Suddenly Jason-Smith grasped my arm and pointed.

'For Chrissake tell me I'm seeing things,' he gasped.

I looked to where he had pointed and was equally astonished. For there, standing majestically on a small mound, waving his walking stick like some frenzied orchestral conductor, was Colonel Joe Soap.

For a moment we stood mesmerised and open-mouthed as we watched him bellowing directions, his eyeglass for once swinging unheeded, his moustache more like that of an angry walrus than ever. Thankfully, we blundered up the beach towards him.

Old Joe looked whacked to the wide. His face was streaked with dirt and lined with fatigue. I was later to learn that somehow he had wangled himself a job as beach-master and had been with the very first wave. When we saw him he had been without sleep for over twenty-four hours, keeping his post, unmoved and unmoveable, through all the worst of the shelling.

We waved furiously to catch his attention. When he saw us

117

he stood still for a moment while he peered forward, fixing his monocle firmly in his eye. Then he said:

'Well done. Well done,' rather like an approving schoolmaster. 'Jason-Smith too. Oh, jolly good. All of you up that track. You'll find it marked. Don't hang about, and keep off the verges. Still mined, you know.'

'Good luck, Sir,' was all we could think of saying.

'And you. And you. Now hurry along. It's a bit safer further up.' He shooed us off, grinning happily. Like Bolton would no doubt have said, 'As happy as a pig in shit'.

It was only after we had plodded up the first kilometre or so of French soil that we were aware of the quiet. Not quiet in the sense that you could hear a pin drop. There were still plenty of bangs going on. A squadron of Spitfires had swept low overhead and a moment later we heard the chatter of their guns as they opened up on the uncomfortably close enemy positions. The difference was that at the beach-head we had been forced to shout at each other. Now, suddenly, we found that, although we were still shouting, this was unnecessary. We could talk conversationally again. The sensation was rather like what a deaf man might feel if he were suddenly to hear a bird sing.

It was during this first moment of relative calm that I realized that, far from being *le beau sabreur*, setting off happily to war with a song on my lips as I had imagined, I'd been as taut as a bowstring. My initial reaction was a wave of almost estatic relief. This was followed swiftly, in the pit of my stomach, by the first throb of fear, which lasted pretty well all the way until Jumbo and I finally managed to find our unit and report to the Commanding Officer.

Shortly before, we had parted from Jason-Smith at rear HQ.

'Remember,' he had said as we bade each other God speed, 'none of that running round trying to capture General Fritz all on your own like you did that time in Northumberland.'

'Like *we* did in Northumberland,' I reminded him. 'Remember now that you're an officer and a gentleman, so always let your men go first.'

'I'll remember.'

He didn't. He was killed a week later leading his tank troop in an attempt to break out of the bridgehead in the offensive against Caen.

Jumbo and I landed up with our new unit at around five o'clock that evening. The rather nice Commanding Officer was from one of the Lancer regiments and a little bit bewildered to find himself in command of three squadrons of the Royal Armoured Corps, most of whom had long since lost their original territorial or regimental distinction.

'Never served in the desert, I suppose?' he greeted us, already resigned to an answer in the negative. 'Never mind. You'll find we're a jolly decent bunch.' Looking round, vaguely hopeful, he added, 'Didn't bring any tanks with you, I suppose?'

'Replacement tanks are expected tomorrow, Colonel,' the Second-in-Command reminded him helpfully. 'Oh. And a water truck.'

'Bloody silly,' said the Colonel. 'Getting the water truck knocked out, I mean. Driver pulled up to have a piddle and ran over a mine. Rather spoilt his matrimonial chances too, I gather.'

While listening to this account of the battalion's disasters, I glanced round the area occupied by HQ. Suddenly my eyes lit on a figure reclining comfortably on one elbow under an apple tree. Although at a distance the pose was not unreminiscent of a bored Cambridge undergraduate idly watching the progress of a cricket match on Fenners, nevertheless the form was unmistakable. When he saw I had spotted him he raised his free hand in a not unfriendly greeting.

'God,' I exclaimed involuntarily to Jumbo, 'guess who?'

'Who?'

'Bolton.'

'God,' said Jumbo in turn.

'One of yours?' asked the Second-in-Command. 'Just been deciding what to do with him. Says he has something wrong with his spine and can't sit in cramped spaces—like in a tank.'

I groaned. Bolton had risen to his feet and was ambling towards us. He attempted an apology for a salute.

'What's this about not being able to sit in a tank?' I asked, trying to keep the sarcasm out of my voice.

'It's the truth, Sir,' he said. 'Took a nasty tumble on the boat coming over. Reckon I've ricked me back something cruel.'

'Well, you'd better report sick, hadn't you?'

Here he took on that cunning look I had come to know so well. 'Don't want to let anyone down, Sir. Did I hear summat about a water truck? Reckon I could drive a water truck OK.'

Before I could get a word in the Second-in-Command had risen to the fly like a starving trout.

'What's that he said? Drive the water truck. Capital. Save me pulling out one of a tank crew. All right as a driver you say? Right, report to the RQMS at stand-to tomorrow.'

'Yes, Sir,' said Bolton. 'I'll do my best, Sir.' He saluted and sloped off, but not before favouring me with another of his lop-sided grins.

'Good man that, I'd say. Made of the right stuff,' said the Colonel.

I groaned inwardly, but at least the fear had left me for a bit. Everything seemed so very normal. Rather like an exercise in England with a few thunderflashes going off every now and again. I spent the night, by courtesy of my new Squadron Commander, in an improvised bivouac behind his tank.

'Better safe than sorry,' he informed me. 'The Hun started to find our range this afternoon. Reckon he'll start up early again tomorrow. Anyway, when we get the replacement tanks we'll be out of here and into Caen before you can say Jack Robinson.'

Optimism is an essential ingredient in a real war and ignorance of what the future might hold one of the greatest blessings. My old Brigadier and R. H. Naylor of the *News of the World* would have been quite out of their depth.

Next day I took over my new troop and found myself proudly mounted in a brand-new Churchill tank. I was just getting to know my command when, towards teatime, I was suddenly faced with my first real front-line crisis. It took the shape of the arrival of a dispatch rider bouncing over the rutted ground to inform me that my presence at regimental HQ was urgently required.

'Christ,' I thought. 'I can't have cocked things up yet.' This automatic feeling of guilt when summoned to the presence of higher authority was, I think, common to all ranks.

'Sutherland,' said the Colonel, as soon as I arrived, rather shaken by a bone-rattling lift on the back of the DR's Norton, 'this fellow of yours, Trooper Bolton.' (How I had wished over the years that people would not automatically describe Trooper Bolton as 'mine'.) 'Picked up the new water truck at 1000 hours this morning. Of course the bloody fools back there had sent it up without any water. Bolton went off to find some and hasn't been seen since.'

He looked at his watch. 'That's over seven hours ago. Good God,' he exploded, 'the whole bloody bridgehead is only about two miles deep. Don't suppose the fellow has got himself blown up do you?'

Why the Colonel should think I had any special knowledge of Bolton's propensity for getting himself blown up I really couldn't imagine.

'Most awkward,' commented the Second-in-Command, stroking his moustache. 'You know what the chaps are about their char. Quite a lot of them are short already.' He shook his head sadly. One felt it would have been less of a disaster if they had run out of ammunition.

I think we might have stood there half the night, shifting awkwardly from foot to foot, if Bolton had not chosen that moment to appear out of the trees, revving his engine and executing a series of racing gear changes before skidding to a halt about a yard from where we were standing.

'Bolton!' I yelled. 'Where the hell . . . ?' Then I stopped short, remembering with relief that I was no longer his CO. It was none of my business. Let him talk himself out of this one alone. He'd had plenty of experience.

'Had a job getting filled up, did you?' said the CO, whom I was later to learn was always one to see the best in everybody. 'Fancy those clots sending it up empty. Got it filled OK?'

Bolton gave him the thumbs-up sign. I had the distinct impression he was rather more than pissed.

'Bit of difficulty, Sir,' he slurred.

'Hope it's all right to drink?' enquired the Colonel.

Bolton climbed out of his cab, mug in hand, went to the rear of the truck and turned the tap on. Then he handed the full mug to the Colonel.

'Looks fine to me,' the Colonel said and putting his head back indulged in a long draught.

The scene which followed needed the genius of H. E. Bateman to do it full justice.

To say that the CO spluttered would have been a considerable understatement. His already seasoned complexion turned a deeper shade of puce. Smoke came out of his ears while his whole six-foot frame was wracked by a paroxsysm of coughing. With one shaking hand he held out the mug to me; his other hand beat the air in a desperate effort to regain his breath.

I sniffed the contents gingerly and even that made my eyes water.

'Bolton! What the hell is this?'

'Local brew, Sir. Made of apples. Managed to liberate a factory all on my own.' He was as proud as if he had won the war single-handed.

It was indeed Calvados, one of France's most delightful liqueurs when matured and yellow with age. This stuff could only have stopped being apples for a week or so and must have been well over 100 per cent proof—all four hundred gallons of it.

Not for the first time Bolton had gone far too far. But on this occasion I felt sure he had finally plunged into the abyss.

I looked at the Colonel, waiting for the explosion. He was smiling seraphically and his eyes had that faraway look.

'Schplendid,' he was saying. 'Ab-sol-ute-ly schplendid. Told you he was a good man, whatsch-his-name.'

I led Bolton quietly back to his truck before the Colonel could embrace him.

In the end we did a deal with a Canadian unit next door. Every day we supplied them with a couple of jerry cans of Bolton's firewater. In return they supplied the needs of the whole battalion with the stuff for making tea and washing behind the ears.

It was an arrangement which lasted for many arduous days while we struggled in vain to progress further in the conquest of Europe. And it was to see us safely through the Great Storm, the final conquest of Caen and the triumphant helter-skelter along the Pas de Calais.

CHAPTER 11

The perceptive reader who has persevered this far will have realized that this memoir is not intended to make any great contribution to a final assessment of the strategies which resulted, somehow or another, in the Allies achieving ultimate victory. It would, however, be apposite at this stage to give a brief account of the situation in which I now found myself, especially as it related to what the higher military rank were inordinately fond of calling 'the bigger picture'.

The peace which had descended upon us once we had left the buggers' muddle on the beaches was entirely misleading. That the scene was not quite as pastoral as it had at first appeared was initially evident in the shape of dead cows and verges marked '*Achtung Minen!*', with accompanying skull and crossbones. But that the enemy were densely populating the countryside little more than the lob of a mortar shell away was not all that forcibly brought to our notice until we had reached our positions.

The dead animals were in a way more horrifying than the dead people I had seen on the beaches. One of the pleasanter aspects of the desert campaign must have been the almost total absence of non-military objectives, whether they were cattle or people and their possessions unfortunate enough to find themselves in the path of war.

(Incidentally, I have often wondered how those '*Achtung Minen!*' signs got there in the first place. Surely they were not put there by the Germans as a friendly warning, and equally surely not left by mistake? Perhaps somebody found them discarded in a ditch and set them up again. Whatever the reason for their appearance, I was to see the warning in German many more times before the match was over.)

What became abundantly apparent after a couple of nights of sleeping under my tank was that the Colonel's confident assumption that, with his Battalion reinforced, we would sweep smoothly forward on our way to Berlin was a little on the optimistic side. We were, in fact, hemmed into a narrow strip, at places scarcely five miles from the landing beaches. Indeed, we were so closely confined that rear HQ was almost in the front line.

The Americans, whose First Army had landed further to the west, had found themselves equally strongly opposed and had suffered even heavier casualties than we had. There were, however, comforting rumours that they were making some progress and there was a strong chance that a link-up with our right flank was imminent. And comfort was something we badly needed on the left flank where we remained firmly pinned to the ground. Certainly there had been a flurry of excitement when we heard that General 'Windy' Gale's paratroopers had given the enemy a bloody nose on the other side of the River Orne close to the coast. To balance up the profit and loss account, however, there was the disastrous attempt by the 7th Armoured Division to join up with the Americans to take the little township of Villers Bocage and so outflank our own objective of Caen. When their 27-ton Cromwell tanks leading the attack ran into a force of German 55-ton Tigers, the Great Umpire in the Sky waved his stick and all the Cromwells fell down.

In our sector, where the original intention had been to launch a frontal attack on Caen itself, the Germans had dug their tanks in so that these became to all intents and purposes heavily-armoured pillboxes with lethal 88mm guns. All attempts to move them proved abortive and when, finally, we overran their positions it was to find that many incredibly brave Germans had died by their guns—most of them looking as if they were scarcely old enough to start shaving.

So we remained more or less sedentary, letting off our guns whenever opportunity offered and predictably receiving salvoes in return, while the ground gained could be measured in terms of a few hundred yards. How long this state of affairs lasted was impossible to gauge. Day simply following night, punctuated by meal times, times for a bit of target practice, and times for a snatch of sleep.

According to the history books the Great Storm started on 19 June, so we must have been sitting on our arses for about ten days. When the wind started to blow it took everybody by surprise, including—or perhaps especially—the meteorologists. Soon the Channel was whipped into torment and enormous breakers dashed against the improvised breakwaters creating indescribable chaos. Even the huge cement blocks which had been towed across the Channel to form Mulberry Harbour were shifted before they had time to settle. The American beach of Omaha suffered the worst, although after three days of unprecedented gales the whole of the landing area was strewn with matchstick wreckage.

Some tank crew reinforcements who joined us immediately after the gale had had the misfortune to make the crossing while the storm was in progress and in consequence had been forced to remain at sea until it blew itself out. They spent their first twenty-four hours ashore alternately throwing up or squatting down.

As far as we were concerned, the great gale had two effects. Firstly, it ran us pretty low on ammunition and other supplies;

secondly, it had given the Germans a respite which they used to fortify further their positions in depth. I believe that, had they chosen at this point to make a serious armoured counter-attack, we would have been in quite serious trouble.

As it was, it was Monty who came in for most of the trouble. Only with reluctance did his critics, and there were many at this point, absolve him from blame for allowing the storm to occur in the first place. However, it now gave them renewed grounds for criticizing his failure not to have taken Caen already and spread out to command the flat and indefensible Caen-Falaise plain on the other side of the River Orne.

The Air Force were particularly pissed off with the performance of the Army and, one must concede, with some reason. Their main complaint was the lack of landing grounds—which the Falaise plains could have provided—and the impossibility of defending such a narrow strip of land in the event of serious opposition from the air. To add to their problems, the air space above the battlefield was almost as congested as the ground below. Particularly to suffer were the tiny Austers, which frequently had to fly through our own barrages, especially those from the battle fleet which we on the ground found so comforting. Such was the density of these barrages, with shells passing over at heights of several thousand feet, that collisions were inevitable—to the distinct disadvantage of the aeroplane.

While Monty could ride, with his customary aplomb, much of the criticism of his colleagues, of whom the most persistent was Air Marshal Tedder who was Deputy Supreme Commander to Eisenhower, the fact remained that he had not fulfilled his promise to deliver Caen into Allied hands on D-Day. The stubborn defence of this desirable objective had taken everyone by surprise and, as the days passed, the failure to take the town assumed ever greater importance as a propaganda weapon in the hands of the anti-Monty faction.

Whether this state of affairs induced Monty, as soon as the

supply position improved after the storm, to switch his objective to an attack to establish a bridgehead on the other side of the Odon River, and so surround and cut out the increasingly festering sore that was Caen, I do not know. The fact remains that within a week of the storm blowing itself out, so successful were supply echelons in resuming normal service that it was possible for the first major offensive in the British sector to be launched.

At the same time I also received my first letter from home since the landing, under the circumstances quite an achievement, and not to be belittled by the fact that it was also to be the last for two months.

The assault on the Odon River, code-named 'Epsom', and largely involving the infantry and those odd creatures the Crocodile flame-spouting dragons of the 'funnies' brigade, was to be a particularly bloody and not altogether successful operation. It must be conceded that the Crocodiles were a considerable success, but I still felt bitter resentment that 'my' CDL tanks had not made the trip. I'm aware of some prejudice, but I believe they could have solved the Caen problem in quick time and if they had achieved that alone this would have justified their use many times over. Despite the presence of the Crocodiles, 'Epsom' achieved virtually nothing and it was almost another month before Caen, reduced to little more than a heap of rubble, was finally taken.

The success of Operation 'Goodwood' (why all these race meetings, one wonders, when one of Monty's pet aversions was horse racing?), which was finally to dispose of the Caen problem, was in no small part due to the Canadian Second Corps. My own involvement in it was less glorious.

We were waiting for the order to advance at the outset of the attack when a squadron of Canadian tanks passed through our position. As they went by, the leading troop commander, who was sitting on his turret regardless of all the banging going on, raised his tea mug in greeting. I was to hear later that he had remained seated on his tank, rather than cowering down inside, which anyone with any sense at all would have done, right on to his objective, for which piece of foolhardiness he was deservedly awarded the Victoria Cross.

At the time I wondered if that raised mug might contain a slug of Bolton's magic elixir. It was while this thought was passing through my mind that there was a really quite horrendous bang and I knew no more.

It was a bright spring day. I was back on the banks of the River Deveron in Aberdeenshire, proudly wearing my first pair of knee-breeches. I was rhythmically casting over the rising trout and my favourite uncle was giving a running commentary.

'Don't try to cast too far, boy. Look, there's a good one right in front of you. Put your fly about a foot above his nose. Oh, well done! Now keep hold of him. Keep your line tight. Right, easy does it. Another yard and I'll get the net under him . . .'

As I watched his back, arm straining forward, landing net in hand, the dream faded and I was conscious of the smell of anaesthetic.

'Nothing to worry about,' the young captain in the Medical Corps was saying. 'A bit concussed. Just flesh wounds. Some steel splinters in the scalp. They'll work themselves out in time.'

Then, seeing I had my eyes open, he remarked conversationally: 'Got a bit of a headache, old son? Just lie there a bit. Don't worry. We'll have you back on the road in no time.'

I shut my eyes again abruptly. To hell with all that, I thought. I want to go back to the banks of the Deveron.

In fact the MO was being optimistic, or maybe just encouraging. By the time I was pronounced fit for duty my lot had rumbled through the ruins that had been Caen and were confidently swanning off in the direction of Berlin.

For more than a month almost a million men had been cooped up on a strip of land so narrow as to make the trip from the front line to rear HQ a matter of a leisurely stroll. For quite a time before a shell had done its bouncing act on my tank turret, everyone had been getting a trifle uptight. *Bonhomie* was wearing thin. So the seven thousand tons of high explosive that had been dumped on Caen in the build-up to the final assault had been music to our ears. At last the boil would be lanced and we would erupt into the clear French air and the rolling countryside. To many of us it almost seemed that the fall of Caen would signal the beginning of the end of the war.

During my temporary incapacity, however, it had not happened that way. The battle for the Orne River had taken place, where my briefly-adopted regiment had earned high honour, but with heavy casualties. In all about 400 tanks had been blown up in the Caen holocaust and my regiment had suffered badly. The trouble had been that the enemy were not, as expected, conducting a tactical withdrawal '*pour mieux sauter*' but were still intent on driving us back into the sea. Attack was met with counter-attack. The roar of guns, the crackling of spandau fire, the sinister whistling of the dreaded, but relatively ineffective, Moaning Minnies, all added up to a dreadful and never-ending cacophony of death and destruction.

By the time I got back into the picture my briefly-joined battalion had ceased to exist. It was a time for re-grouping.

Now the name of Falaise was on everyone's lips as the 'New Jerusalem'. 'Close the Falaise Gap and we have them,' we were told, I am not sure by whom. Once again in reserve, sitting in a pleasant enough tent with a dozen or so similarly placed officers, nobody told us anything. Higher Command had other things to think of than relieving the boredom of a handful of odds and sods. We were for the time all dressed up with nowhere to go, while others in front ploughed painfully ahead.

And that is how it remained while July moved into August

and the opening day of the grouse shooting season came and went. Was old Clark, the family gardener, still alive and ready with his loaded shotgun by his cottage door? 'Home' seemed a hundred years ago. Although I filled in the odd moment by scribbling notes to all and sundry, our little group did not appear to be in any postal area and remained incommunicado until we caught up with a few sacks of letters in Brussels. Nor, I later discovered, did many of my own letters ever arrive.

Around the end of August we at last received orders to move. We formed a small group mounted in some brand-new scout cars. They were little, lightly-armoured boxes but sturdy and nippy enough with a driver and gunner/wireless operator. My last troop of Churchill tanks had been more or less shot from under me before I had really got to know many of the crews. Now, driven in some state by ex-professional boxer Jock Lewis, and with cockney 'know-all' Bert Brigstocke (Brigsy) as gunner, we set off in convoy to try to catch up with the war.

This was to prove an horrific experience. There was not a copse, not a thicket, which did not house its quota of mangled dead. The roadsides were lined with them and in the fields the grotesquely bloated bodies of farm animals, their stiffened legs pointing to the sky, lay like children's toys thrown carelessly aside.

Driving through the carnage which was the Falaise Gap (known journalistically as the Falaise 'pocket'), it was impossible to avoid seeing the dead, their bodies and faces caught in the grotesque posturing of broken puppets. To glance with professional interest at a 'brewed-up' Tiger or Panther tank in order to assess the manner of its disablement was to see the torso of the driver half out of his escape hatch or the mangled remains of the commander sprawled on top of the turret. In the Falaise 'pocket' there were many who, like the brave German defenders of Caen, looked as if they hadn't started to shave yet.

Although there were still pockets of resistance in places such as Le Havre, or, more important, the Pas de Calais, where the Germans had always expected the main assault and kept it highly defended with their Panzer divisions, our little pocketful of temporary freelancers were headed for Rouen where Joan of Arc had, so recently in the memories of all true French, been burned at the stake by the perfidious English.

As we entered the outskirts of the cathedral city we were acutely aware of our role as imposters. After all, *we* had not liberated Rouen, and yet as we drove into the main square we were pelted with flowers and greeted with screams of adulation. There were Union Jacks everywhere. Where the hell did they come from? Young—and not so young—ladies clambered on to the top of our scout cars, offering *everything*.

'Fuck me,' came Jock's voice from the obscurity of the driver's seat, 'don't I get a look in?'

After the horrors of what we had witnessed on the drive, I think we had all been so beset by misery that we had forgotten that we, too, were people and alive.

'Jock,' I said, calling him by his first name for the first time and initiating a relationship which was to survive many a trial, 'so long as you do not wish me personally to oblige you in the matter, I think that there will be plenty of opportunity shortly. In the meantime keep your eyes on the bloody road.'

We parked our cars under the trees in the square. Immediately scores of children clambered all over our vehicles, begging to be allowed to sit in the driver's seat or to peer through the periscope. With difficulty we locked the hatches and made a dash for the nearest bistro. After all, a locked armoured car is almost child-proof and for some time I had been missing the stimulation of Bolton's water truck.

I don't think any of us paid for a drink the whole time we were in Rouen. Everyone was anxious to regale us with stories of '*les sales Boches*'. Overnight all the youth had become freedom

fighters, and if some of them appeared to protest their patriot-
ism overmuch, surely that was only natural. Only the elder
statesmen sat quietly at their regular tables, clad in their best
suits and playing their eternal games of tric-trac or boule. Every
now and again one of them would signal to *le patron* and yet
another glass of cognac would appear at our elbows. Across the
smoke-laden room glasses would be raised in a mutual toast
and the old men would smile gently. They had seen it all before.

There was, however, an uglier side to this euphoric atmosphere of good will. In the streets we would frequently come
across gangs of youths, obviously bent on trouble and not too
particular where they found it. A glimpsed figure and the cry
'*collaborateur!*' would go up. Then they'd be off like a pack of
hounds baying for blood. Not a few private scores were settled
by this form of lynch law, not least against the ladies of the town
accused of selling their bodies to the Germans. Many had their
heads shaved and not a few their clothes removed for good
measure while the more law-abiding citizens, including the
gendarmerie, stood by.

We had received no particular instructions, except that we
were to be reserves for an independent tank brigade and if
anyone became dead we would be called upon to jump into the
breach, the exact nature of which was left unspecified. Looking
back now, nearly forty years later, it is difficult to grasp just how
little any of us knew about what was going on. All we had to rely
on was rumour. Monty, it was rumoured, was in the middle of
one of his spats with Ike, which was a matter of indifference to
us, although our money was generally speaking on Monty. We
had heard vaguely that the Americans had got fed up toiling
over the Italian Alps and that General Mark Clark had moved
their field of operations to the south of France, where they had
landed without a great deal of opposition. Not without envy, we
assumed they would have commandeered all the brothels and
that that was the last we would hear of that particular army.

There were also rumours that our job would be to make a mad dash for Brussels where, no doubt, we would attempt to emulate the supposed American successes.

Motoring in the wake of the dogged advance along the north coast of France there were the odd moments of excitement, such as when we almost caught up with the action in the Pas de Calais and one independently-minded tank gunner loosed off a number of rounds of rapid fire at the deserted emplacements from which the notorious doodle-bugs had been launched against London. His mum, he explained apologetically, had been killed in the London blitz and he had acted in a fit of temper. Everyone clicked their tongues sympathetically.

All seemed to be going quite well until suddenly, with the Belgian border in sight, the whole force to which we were loosely attached was put into a state of suspended animation. We were literally stopped in our tracks, a state of affairs simply achieved by an order from on high that we were to have no more petrol supplies. The reason was that the Americans, who had had much the bloodiest time at the landings but who had since experienced a relatively easy passage on their way to Paris, had not yet reached their destination and, it was understood, we must jolly well wait where we were until they did.

So, with supplies of petrol finally spluttering out on the Belgian border, the only thing to do was to find as comfortable a billet as possible, embark on a spot of fraternization with the local population and enjoy ourselves as best we could.

I had acquired a small Volkswagen and just enough petrol to do a bit of swanning around the countryside. Brigsy and Jock had 'liberated' the car somewhere and reconditioned it. It was not seemly, I had informed them, that other ranks should ride around in motor cars while their betters were dismounted. So, in turn, I 'liberated' it from them.

The nearest town of any size was Lille, but on occasions I got as far as such cultural centres as Rheims, which had not only contributed a fine cathedral to the civilized world but also introduced '*la méthode champagnoise*', thus translating the very dull local white wine into that splendid liquid which the Edwardians, rather unhygienically one feels, used to quaff out of actresses' slippers.

To my joy I discovered that Jumbo, whom I had last seen trudging up the beach in Normandy, had also become dehorsed and was in much the same place and situation as myself. With more mixed feelings I also learned that Bolton had attached himself to Jumbo's lot. I should have known better, but at the reunion celebrations I introduced Bolton to Jock and Brigsy.

A day or two later a most curious incident occurred. Jumbo and I were doing a bit of personal reconnoitring in a part of the country not known for its scenic attractiveness. However, when we came to a coppice through which a stream gurgled quite merrily, we decided to take a stroll.

Teetering between boredom and frustration and having long since exhausted the more commonplace conversational gambits, Jumbo remarked, pointing to the .38 Smith and Wesson revolver on my belt, which it is compulsory for every officer to carry on all occasions under pain of the direst retribution, 'I suppose that amongst your many military accomplishments you are a deadly revolver shot?'

'Deadly,' I agreed modestly. 'In fact, I believe myself to be amongst the finest revolver shots in the entire British Army.'

'In that case,' said Jumbo, pointing to a line of low spruce trees along our path and behind a higher bank of leafy hardwoods, 'perhaps you would draw your weapon and just shoot the bud off the top of that small fir tree.'

Never one to duck a challenge, particularly if it involved me in no personal danger or discomfort, I withdrew the weapon from my belt, took careful aim and fired. The bud remained unshaken but a moment later there came the most fearful crash.

We brushed our way through the scrub and there, flat on his back, arms and legs in the air like a large beetle, lay a German soldier in camouflaged battledress. He was quite dead, hit between the eyes, and obviously one of the rearguard of snipers who tied themselves into trees waiting for an opportunity to have a crack at the enemy before escaping. I would like to think he was about to have a pot-shot at us but since his ropes were untied and he was quite a way behind the lines, he was probably just seeking a chance to escape. In which case it was jolly bad luck.

Soon we heard that it was not us but the Guards who were to be given the very pleasant task of liberating an undefended Brussels, the Americans, in the meantime, having made it to Paris. From the chorus of loud groans all round on receiving this news, the only abstainers were Jock, Brigsy and Bolton who, literally, were as merry as thieves. They had formed an unholy triumvirate and so far as I could discover had already 'liberated' two motor cycles and a forty-seater bus of German origin which they had flogged to the local mayor.

Therefore it was perhaps unfortunate for them that at this time the powers that be decided to strike a blow against, among other things, the prevalent practice of black marketeering. This measure took the form of withdrawing all currency in circulation, which had to be declared at the bank and exchanged for distinctively different notes, called British Liberation Army Vouchers (known as BLAVs). This action was a sore blow to both the French and Belgians, who have a marked disinclination to pay income tax and are accustomed, even in peacetime, to keep very large sums of money, including that which has been legally obtained, under their mattresses.

The wailing and gnashing of teeth among the local population was heartrending to behold. So serious was their predicament that certain of the more honest traders were having to hitch a dray horse to a cart in order to transport their accumulated funds to the bank. Trooper Bolton and his fellow conspirators had, of course, been paid for their various transactions in the old currency, now about to become as much use as the piece of paper Neville Chamberlain had brought back from Germany in 1938. Personally, I fell about laughing.

However, Bolton and his chief lieutenant, 'I know it all' Brigstocke, were made of sterner stuff. It so happened that I was at the time in charge of the unit's Imprest Account, through which all the unit's funds passed. This meant that at times I held, very properly, quite considerable sums of money in hand drawn from the Field Paymaster. At other times, after payday for example, I had very little. Conveniently, the Field Paymaster had to cash in old notes in possession of the troops and issue BLAVs.

Of course, serving a whole division, he had no idea what money stocks any of his customers possessed. Nevertheless, I think he must have had an inkling that something was a bit fishy when Jumbo and I dumped an embarrassingly large trunk of old notes on his desk: after all, the mayor himself had thrown in quite a bit of his own slush fund. However, he carried out the transaction with all the poker-faced efficiency of his banking breed.

The mayor was so grateful that he offered us a share of the proceeds; but we felt, as officers and gentlemen, obliged to refuse. Instead, Jumbo and I accepted a case of twenty-four very small bottles of black Belgian beer which the mayor claimed was some incredible number of years old. '*Ne buvez pas de trop*,' he said, wagging a finger before embracing us warmly.

We took it back to the mess and finished off the lot between about eight of us—three bottles each. Or did some of us have more than others? The only thing I remember was that just before midnight we received orders to move: reveille, 0430 hours, move off 0530 hours. But it was not until well after 0500 that any officer actually got his head off the pillow.

Never in the history of human endeavour can any set of officers have advanced to give battle with less enthusiasm.

CHAPTER 12

'Well, hungover or not, here we go again,' I thought to myself, as Jumbo and I climbed, bleary-eyed, into my liberated Volkswagen. It still bore, if not German markings, at least German-type camouflage. As such it was neither fish, flesh nor fowl and attracted little attention from either side, as we were to discover.

Not yet officially posted to any unit, we were reserve troops of an independent armoured brigade commanded by a charming old warrior, whom I was later to come to know well and who went, for some reason, by the nickname of 'Wahoo'.

Our role was to pass through the Guards battalion having their will with the population of Brussels, turn north to the sadly-bombed port of Antwerp and trundle up into Holland. Part of the advance force had the bad luck to be involved in splashing around in the flooded area of Walcheren, where there was some very nasty and muddy fighting. Luckily, we were on the other flank.

With the reserve unit duly installed just over the Dutch border, Jumbo and I decided that we deserved a night off. So, granting ourselves an unofficial 48-hour pass, we set off back to Antwerp for a few jars of most excellent Belgian beer and to sample what other touristic 'attractions' the night life of that sea port might have to offer.

Just before sun-up on the following morning, with the experiences of the previous night having fully lived up to our great expectations, we set off to resume our military duties, both of us rather badly in need of some sleep.

Under the circumstances it was perhaps understandable that it took an hour or so of motoring, with daylight breaking on the forms of industrious Dutch peasants setting out on their day of toil, before we began to experience a distinct feeling that all was not well. Perhaps after I had been forced to swerve sharply to avoid a dead German lying in the middle of the road a tiny doubt should have stirred.

As in England, all road signs which might have helped the invaders had been removed. However, despite our navigational skills, it soon became apparent, as we approached a sizeable town, that a small error in map-reading had occurred. I gave Jumbo a shake and muttered 'Where the hell are we?'

'Just keep on till you see a policeman or someone and ask,' he grumbled and returned to his slumbers.

It was rather a nice town. Arriving in the main square I slowed down to see if I could spot a café where we could have a coffee and maybe a cognac to help us on our way.

Spotting just the right place, I pulled up outside, gave Jumbo a shake and began to open the car door. Then I took a closer look through the steamed-up café windows. The place was full of Germans—live ones. We had somehow or another got a little bit ahead of the game. I closed the door, slipped into gear as quietly as possible and stole away.

I now had Jumbo's full attention. It was really a bit of a problem. This was no time to be taken prisoner, or even worse. Luckily, the car itself would not attract attention, but here we were, imprisoned inside in our British uniforms and without the slightest idea which way to drive. Indeed, to proceed in any direction, even back on the road we had come, was to court disaster. Somebody would be bound to stop and ask ques-

tions—or perhaps shoot first and ask questions afterwards.

Rather pointlessly we took off our berets and battledress blouses. But there was no way we could make ourselves look anything other than what we were—two bleary-eyed British officers in a knocked-off German vehicle.

As we cruised slowly along, we came to a large ecclesiastical building, complete with a cupola reminiscent of St Peter's in Rome. Jumbo suddenly said, 'What religion are you? A bloody Presbyterian, I suppose.'

'Correct. Why?'

'Sanctuary. That's a monastery if I'm not mistaken. Why don't we seek sanctuary? They might even overlook the Presbyterian bit.'

'Sanctuary didn't do Thomas à Becket much good.'

'Dry up.'

A moment later we were across the still happily almost deserted street and banging on the postern gate. After what seemed an eternity a grille slid back and an ancient tonsured head peered out at us.

At moments such as these it is rather difficult to know just what to say. Most phrase books do not cover this type of contingency, and anyway my Dutch is minimal.

In a moment of inspiration I mimed Dürer's 'Praying Hands'. Seconds later the door opened and we were beckoned inside.

The ancient monk's face was wreathed in smiles. In near perfect English he said, 'You have captured the town? *Dei gratia*. Come. Matins are finished. I will take you to the Abbot.'

'I'm afraid we have not taken the town. On the contrary, there is considerable danger that the town will take us,' I responded.

'We are seeking sanctuary,' said Jumbo doggedly.

'I will still take you to the Abbot,' said the custodian of the gate.

The Abbot received us in a book-lined study far removed from my idea of a monastic cell, and equally far removed from my idea of war. He proved to possess great charm, as well as being a highly practical man.

'You must have taken the wrong fork about ten kilometres back. You were unlucky, but your army cannot be far away. We have been expecting them daily.'

We showed him on the map where we were meant to be.

'You will stay here with us until the Germans leave,' he stated decisively. 'I will telephone the Abbé there who will inform your friends that you are safe.'

We did not argue with this man of God. His idea seemed eminently sensible. Having communicated entirely by wireless since the landing, it had not occurred to us that anything so civilized as a telephone might still be working.

We spent the following days playing basketball with the young priests who, in spite of their cumbersome robes, proved extraordinarily agile. We ate sparsely and drank water in the refectory at midday but made up for it by consuming considerable quantities of liqueurs with the Abbot and some of the older priests after evensong.

We also spent a lot of time praying, because we thought it the polite thing to do. Thinking of enough people to pray for wasn't easy but, in addition to my family, I put in a good word for the Royal Family, Winston Churchill, Field-Marshal Montgomery, and for good measure the Moderator of the Church of Scotland. Jumbo also prayed: largely for Watneys and Guinness.

Our abstemious life of cloistered calm came to an end when, on the morning of our fifth day, the sound of sporadic gunfire filtered through and we knew the war had caught up with us again.

We said our good-byes and I like to think the sadness we felt was reciprocated by the Abbot and his men.

As the postern gate closed behind us Jumbo glanced across the road.

'Some bastard has nicked our car,' he said.

Some bastard had. However, despite this heavy loss, like the British troops at Mafeking on that May day some forty-five years previously, we felt extremely relieved.

Shortly after this pleasant interlude orders came through posting most of us to proper regiments. My posting also called for three replacement tank crew, so I naturally picked Jock and Brigsy as driver and wireless operator. It was their idea that Bolton should come along as co-driver. Better the devil you know I thought, resigned to the fact that he had become a permanent fixture in my life.

My new bunch turned out to be a fairly mongrel lot, a hybrid regiment drawn from different bits and pieces of the Royal Armoured Corps and simply designated by a number. Nevertheless, despite our lack of ancient lineage and non-existent battle honours, we were a happy regiment with bags of *esprit de corps*.

The Colonel, who liked to pose as something of a martinet, had some rather quaint ideas and one or two eccentric habits. For example, his most prized possession was his personal lavatory seat—a well-scrubbed wooden affair on which, lest some thief in the night might steal it away, he had had his initials deeply burned with a red-hot poker. I believe that Field-Marshal Montgomery sported a similar model. One of the earliest regimental responsibilities bestowed on me was that of 'Keeper of the Colonel's Seat'. Whenever it was required an orderly would apply to me for it and after use he would return the precious object into my hands for safe-keeping.

Summer was nearly over and we were camping out near Eindhoven, speculating on whether there would be much more offensive action before winter set in. The general feeling was that there would be a new offensive because Monty wanted it all over and done with by Christmas. I had just reluctantly given up my important position as Keeper of the Seat and been posted to 'A' Squadron as a troop commander when there was the most frightful commotion and everyone was ordered to stand-by with engines warmed up ready for instant action.

The Germans, we had been given vaguely to understand, were sticking around somewhere in the area of Nijmegen, but it was not our turn to go chasing after them. Then came the order to move and away we went, taking turns to head north-west with orders to capture a certain bridge over the River Maas if possible.

Ian, my new Squadron Commander, who was to become one of my closest friends, didn't seem a lot wiser when we harboured for the first night. Then the news started to seep through that there had been a huge airborne landing beyond Nijmegen at a place called Arnhem.

'It's going to be our job to link up with them,' declared know-all Brigsy. 'It'll be the beginning of the end, you mark my words.'

We were the leading troop and thus it was that on the next day, quite unopposed, we arrived at our objective. The bridge was intact but, as ordered, I reported back to Ian before making the crossing. Ian reported back to the Colonel, who presumably informed the Brigadier, and so on ever upwards until possibly it came to the ears of the great man himself that Sutherland and his disreputable, thieving bunch were sitting on their arses by the roadside, having the odd game of cards, a bit short of cigarettes as usual, and wanting to know what the hell next.

Eventually, after quite a long wait, the order came. It was to turn round and go back again all the way to Eindhoven. The amateur strategists in my troop were aghast, especially as we were just beginning to fancy ourselves as the triumphant spearhead of the relieving force, sweeping on to final victory, accompanied by Vera Lynn singing 'I'll See You Again'.

Many brave men died at and around Arnhem. But the reason why our own particular participation at that time turned into such a complete non-event, I have never been able to ascertain with any certainty. Anyway, it was back to stables, with a distinct feeling that something had gone badly wrong.

September moved into October, October into November, and we were all comfortably settled in, looking forward to Christmas in Holland. The hospitality of the Dutch was quite extraordinary, equalled only by that of the French and the Belgians.

My little troop consisted of three Churchill tanks, the other two commanded by Sergeant Joe and Lance-Sergeant Wally. I was on first-name terms with most of my lot; only on appropriate occasions did I resort to formality. Mostly they called me 'Sir' to my face; I can only hope that they did not call me anything particularly offensive behind my back.

The festive season was almost upon us; Bolton was prowling round casting covetous eyes at the local farmers' turkeys, geese and daughters, when suddenly the balloon went up again with a vengeance.

General Von Rundstedt, apparently not imbued with the Christmas spirit, had launched a *Blitzkrieg*-type offensive against the American sector and his left-hook attack through the Belgian Ardennes was already threatening to retake Brussels and Antwerp which, incidentally, would have had the effect of putting almost the whole of the British fighting force in the bag. It was not the time to be thinking about turkeys.

Much to the chagrin of General 'Blood and Guts' Patton, who was in command of the US forces, Eisenhower called on Monty to take supreme command to deal with this sudden and totally unexpected menace. This was without doubt Monty's finest hour.

Within minutes we had thrown everything together and had set off for the happy hunting grounds at a rate of knots in the wake of our jubilant Field-Marshal. The speed of our departure may be judged by the fact that in the confusion the Colonel's lavatory seat was left behind and a motor-cyclist had to be sent back to retrieve it before we could join in the battle.

As we rumbled *ventre à terre* out of Holland the scenery improved dramatically, although we were in no real mood to enjoy it, for the weather and the state of the roads deteriorated in inverse proportion to the distance covered. The flat, straight roads of Holland turned into the hilly, twisty and snow-covered death-traps of Belgium.

The Churchill tank—or any tank for that matter—is not at its best in mud and ice. If all 38 tons of it decides to slide, it will continue in its chosen trajectory until it comes up against some immovable object, or more likely plunge over a convenient precipice. The driver's knack is to persuade the beast not to slide, and at this Jock was a master. The two great bunches of bananas that represented his fingers were as sensitive as a piano tuner's. My agonized instructions to him to 'take it easy for

Chrissake!' or 'watch out for that bloody ditch!' were quite unnecessary, although I continued to bombard him with instructions simply to relieve my own tensions.

Wireless operator Brigsy, despite his appalling habit at times of tuning into the BBC instead of the squadron wavelength, more than compensated for this aberration by a remarkable ability to click dead on net when needed. 'Bunny' Austin, the turret gunner and newest member of the crew, had the eyes of a hawk. He often spotted enemy tanks through the restricted vision of his periscope before I did with my head out of the top and all-round vision.

As for Bolton in the co-driver's seat, lazy, scruffy, insubordinate he may have been in hours of ease, but if we cast a track in a six-foot snow drift or he volunteered for any of the unavoidable but dicey jobs such as a foot reconnaissance, then he became as cheerful, efficient and determined as the most highly trained and dedicated professional—in a highly unprofessional way!

Although my memory may have become somewhat rose-coloured with the passage of time, I am certain that as far as my troop was concerned—and my crew in particular—the more bloody the conditions and the greater the danger, the more splendidly efficient they became. Broadly speaking, I can say the same about most of those with whom I was closely associated in battle.

We slipped and slithered our way to Dinant, a charming old hugger-mugger of a Belgian town and not for the first time in its long history a place of key importance, commanding as it does one of the main crossing places of the fast-flowing, steep-sided river bed of the Meuse. Eventually, apart from a few hair-raising moments on the road, we arrived, happily parked our diesel-hungry, mud-caked tanks, and were told to fall out and find what accommodation we could for the night.

I don't know quite what we had expected. Perhaps to be plunged straight away into a desperate defence of the vital Meuse valley, the last strong defensive feature before Brussels and the Channel Ports. In fact, the only troops we had encountered had been black Americans driving supply trucks and the only signs of enemy activity the by now unusual sight of German fighter planes swooping menacingly overhead.

It was at times like these that I found Bolton at his most caring. I was fussing about trying to find a billet for my lot when Bolton, who had as usual absented himself from the more routine chores such as refuelling, suddenly reappeared with a most delectable dark-haired beauty of perhaps thirty summers, give or take a summer or two.

'Found you a billet for the night,' he announced, tapping me on the shoulder.

The lady, it appeared, wished to provide free accommodation. The reason for Bolton's unselfishness, as it had a habit of doing, became blindingly clear when I discovered that she had room for a single brave soldier and was only prepared to extend her patriotic gesture to a member of the officer class. But it would have been churlish to refuse. And who was I to grumble? I could, however, have done without Bolton's Parthian shot before he sloped off again:

'I can find my own bit of tail,' he shrugged.

Such amorous adventures have always been regarded as spoils of war. An hour later, soaking in a steaming hot bath while through the open door came the comforting sounds of a candlelit meal for two in course of preparation, the menace of von Rundstedt and his Panzer divisions somewhere out in the snowy waste was infinitely remote.

Suddenly there was a violent hammering on the door of the small apartment. 'My God,' I thought, involuntarily clutching a face flannel to my private parts. 'A cuckolded husband? A double-crossed lover? Even perhaps a German storm-trooper?'

It was none of these. It was Trooper Bolton, standing in the bathroom doorway and smiling his lop-sided grin at my discomfiture.

'Bad luck, Sir,' he said. 'Orders to stand to and be ready to move off in half an hour to occupy the high ground over the river.'

In my hurry I even forgot to make a note of the lady's address for possible future reference.

That night, which had augured so well, turned into what was without doubt the coldest I have ever endured. Sleep was impossible. Any heat that could be derived from lying on the engine hatches soon evaporated. Instead, to touch the steel hull with a bare hand was to risk the skin sticking frozen to the metal. To start engines was against orders. So we spent the night battened down in shivering wakefulness, brewing tea at intervals on a primus stove—equally against rules but less easy to detect.

There was some desultory discussion as to where the hell the Americans were and some interest in what dawn would reveal when it broke. When at last it grew light enough to see, the first things we could make out were some corpses by a hedge to our right front, so covered in frosted rime as to make their uniforms unrecognizable. Only their steel helmets proclaimed that they were German.

The days that followed were, to put it mildly, both confused and confusing. In the Ardennes open and closely-wooded countryside occur in almost equal proportion. The general information was that the enemy offensive had been halted, but it was not clear that all German units were aware of this. What was certain was that they were still thick on the ground in parts and that a large contingent of US troops was cut off in the area of Bastogne some fifty miles to the south-west. As it turned out, the stubborn defence of Bastogne by the Americans was to be one of the most gallant (and least reported) actions of the war in

Europe. Our job at the time was to press on as fast as the enemy would permit and relieve our beleagured Allies.

We dodged our way forward across the frozen countryside, keeping to the fields which, being frozen hard, made for good going and avoided the possibility of mined roads and verges. From time to time we caught sight of disorganized groups of the enemy, their grey uniforms showing up sharply against the snow-covered ground. Bolton rattled off a few rounds of Besa fire at them but they showed no inclination for a scrap. It certainly seemed that the Germans were on the run.

On the second morning, however, cautiously approaching some heavy cover, the ever-watchful Bunny shouted, 'Hold everything, take a look at the left-hand corner of the trees.' Instinctively Jock slewed the tank behind a rather sparse hedge and I burbled a warning over the 'B' set to Joe and Wally, who followed suit.

Peering through my field glasses I spotted the unmistakable muzzle of a German Tiger tank's 88mm gun poking out from under the bare branches. The hull of the tank was out of view,

so presumably we had not been spotted. Peradventure they sleepeth, I thought.

We edged forward up the hedge in single file until within perhaps 500 yards. The muzzle of the 88mm continued to stare straight ahead and remained quite motionless, not swinging from side to side looking for a target as was usual. It could have been a dummy but we were taking no chances. Simultaneously we all three fired armour-piercing shells into the bushes. There was a moment's complete silence then a terrific bang followed by an explosion of smoke and flame. A moment later the crew came tumbling out with their hands up, except for one who was still trying to pull up his trousers.

Incredibly they had all been out of their tank stretching their legs, answering the various calls of nature preparatory to joining the withdrawal.

And so day by day we slithered and stumbled forward. Although we were met with occasional defiant bursts of spandau fire, which tinkled noisily but harmlessly against our hulls, we encountered no more German tanks.

One afternoon we ran into an American infantry unit plodding determinedly over fences and ditches which we in our tanks could take easily and without discomfort. I pulled up, dismounted, and went over to say hello and offer them a lift on the engine hatches. I myself had taken to travelling almost exclusively outside on the hatches to combat the extreme cold.

'Sit on the back of one of those Goddam matchboxes? Hell no!' said the American lieutenant. He was a cheerful fellow who, by the look of him, had seen some pretty hard service. As we were standing together passing the time of day, chatting amiably and exchanging good-natured insults about the relative merits of our national fighting abilities, some trigger-happy Kraut chose to open fire.

We both dived for cover in opposite directions. I landed in a shallow ditch right on top of an American GI who had beaten me to it.

'Oh my luck!' he exclaimed, with exaggerated affectation. 'A gorgeous *man*—and an *officer* at that!'

It was my first never-to-be-forgotten meeting with Bob. We were next to meet when we were staff officers both attending the Nuremberg War Crimes trial as observers. By that time he was an officer himself with a row of gallantry decorations and we were to become firm friends. The Ardennes was the beginning of my admiration for the American fighting soldier.

After what seemed never-ending days spent surviving the arctic conditions, it was with utmost relief that one evening we finished up in a small village offering every prospect of a night with a roof over our heads.

I contacted the local vicar, who was a Protestant, and arranged for my troop to take over the church hall.

'You, of course, will be my personal guest,' he said hospitably.

Arriving at the vicarage I was introduced to the vicar's family, consisting of Mama and an assortment of children, of whom the most striking was an 18-year-old called Louise. Then I was shown my room and urged to take a much-needed bath, smelling as I did of burnt mud and diesel oil. The family had already supped early as was their custom. One of the servants was to bring me a meal in my room, since the rest of the household were off to the church to attend a thanksgiving service for their deliverance.

Bathed and refreshed I was relaxing on the bed when, to my surprise, it was Louise herself who appeared with my supper on a tray. It appeared that the vicar considered the servants more in need of spiritual uplift than his own daughter.

She handed me the tray, settled herself in a chair, and we started to chat. When I had finished bolting down the food she suddenly remarked,

'Your French is not very good. I will give you a lesson if you would care.'

I must admit to being somewhat surprised, personally considering my French to be quite excellent. However, I was always ready to learn something new—especially from such a pretty teacher.

Seating herself beside me on the end of the narrow bed, she took my hand in hers and putting it to her head said, as if to a child,

'*La tête*. The head.'

'*La tête*. The head,' I repeated, humouring her.

'*Les oreilles*. The ears,' she said, first tugging one of her ears and then one of mine.

'*Les yeux*. The eyes,' she said, opening hers wide.

'*Les yeux*. The eyes,' I replied, opening mine even wider.

'*La bouche.*'

'*La bouche*. The mouth,' I repeated.

'*Les épaules*. The shoulders.'

This was really beginning to take off.

When we had got as far as '*la poitrine*; *elles sont deux*,' and I had to place my hand on each of these delectable parts of her anatomy in turn, my mind was away ahead of the game.

'*L'estomac*,' she said, grasping my hand and performing a circular movement. 'How you say in English "*L'estomac*"?'

'The stomach,' I stammered, hardly able to wait for what was to come next.

What was to come next was a knock at the door.

'*Ma'm'selle*,' said a voice urgently, '*Ton père te cherche. Viens vite!*'

She put her finger to her lips. '*Je reviendrai*,' she promised, rather like General MacArthur had remarked to the Japanese. But unlike the General I did not see her again, although I kept a late vigil before fatigue overtook me.

The following morning, when I came to bid my host and

hostess good-bye at the front door, I thought I caught sight of a slight movement of a lace curtain behind a barred upper window; but I could not be sure.

During that night news had come through that Bastogne had been relieved by the Americans—without as far as I was concerned much help from us—and that the crisis was over.

Our participation in the Battle of the Bulge held one further surprise all the same.

Motoring gently back towards the Meuse our energetic second-in-command had gone ahead, scouting for somewhere we could park ourselves as a squadron for once as comfortably as possible pending further orders. He had been so phenomenally successful that we soon found ourselves in an officers' mess, together with bedrooms with private baths *en suite*, in none other than the Château Royale d'Ardennes, arguably one of the most luxurious hotels in Europe.

This was an officers' mess with perfectly trained civilian waiters and boasting a chef of the highest calibre. Right through the war this splendid hotel, although requisitioned in turn by the Germans, the Americans, the Germans again and now the British, had attempted to interpret as literally as possible the slogan 'service as usual'.

We were even required to sign the visitors' book on arrival. I wonder if that book still exists? It surely must be an historic document.

What happened next, as so often in warfare, was precisely nothing. In fact it was Ian's opinion that we would be allowed to sit where we were for some time. So confident was he of this view that he and I got up a party and went into Dinant (I never did find that charming lady's address again), equipped ourselves with skis and provided ourselves with a great deal of fun attempting to break all our limbs as inexpertly as possible.

The Ardennes is a sportsman's paradise and Ian and I, as the only two unashamed blood sportists in the squadron, were determined to take every advantage of this unexpected bonus. I even managed to forget about my frustrated love life. We had both 'liberated' twelve bores at some stage or another and most evenings were spent flighting pigeons, which had reached almost plague proportions in numbers and which provided splendid material for the attention of our expert and ingenious chef.

I had a vague memory of a Belgian baron who had once stayed with my father in Scotland. A diligent search through the local telephone book revealed a name I thought I recognized and so we decided to pay a courtesy call. Armed with a bottle of whisky Ian and I found ourselves motoring up the driveway of what was revealed as a magnificent château set deep in the woods.

As it turned out the baron had never been to Scotland in his life but nevertheless was charm personified. The conversation quickly turned from the war to sport and just as quickly the baron offered to lay on a full-scale boar shoot for our benefit, complete with beaters and all.

The shoot was relatively uneventful as drive after drive went by with only the occasional high pheasant coming over the guns. The war had taken its toll of the game in the Ardennes as everywhere else.

Then, on the last drive of the day, right opposite my stand I heard a great deal of thrashing about in the undergrowth. My finger tightened on the trigger, certain as I was that at any moment an enraged boar was about to burst into the open

There was a sudden parting of the foilage but, instead of a *sanglier* breaking cover and coming like an express train towards us, the Brigade Chaplain strode into view. A thorough muscular Christian, long country rambles were his favourite way of relaxing. How he got mixed up in our shoot I don't know but I hope he never realized how nearly I came to depriving the

Church of one of its greatest theologians and scholars of the post-war years.

It was well into the New Year before we received orders to return to our own cabbage patch. Our sojourn in the Ardennes may have had its moments of frustration but it had also provided a hell of a lot of fun.

It was not until April that we got an inkling of what was next in store for us. And if rumour was not to prove a lying jade, at first sight the news verged on the ludicrous.

When at last the order came to move north again into the Arnhem area we had to go without Bolton. He had managed to contract pneumonia and was carted off to base hospital. His replacement was a likely lad called 'Geordie' Walker.

A pity about Bolton, I found myself thinking. Somehow I'd like him to have been around for what looked like being the finale.

CHAPTER 13

Of course, the whole situation was really too absurd, and in the following forty-eight hours the ludicrousness of it all became ever more apparent.

Squadron commanders were ordered to take their troop commanders, crawling on their bellies, each in turn to a derelict old windmill which, it was alleged, gave a fantastic view of the proposed battlefield. In fact it gave a fantastic view of half a mile or so of pitiless, bare, open ground that sloped down to the Reichswald, one of Europe's densest forests. But the scene was no more panoramic than the one we could have observed lying behind a bush at ground level, without the risk of falling through the rotting woodwork of the windmill staircase or showing ourselves twenty feet up in the air, peering white-faced, our field glasses glinting in the evening sunlight, from the topmost window of the mill.

When we tottered down again from the giddy heights, having survived the traumatic experience and having failed to spot any sign of the enemy, we put our hands in our pockets and strolled off back over the hill to the tank laager area.

'What's doing?' asked Brigsy.

'Sort of covert shoot,' I answered.

'You mean with beaters and all that driving the birds out? Used to do a bit of that with me dad in Hampshire.'

'Much the same,' I told him gently. 'Only in this case we have to get in and beat *them* out.'

'In tanks? In a wood?' said Jock. 'Fuck me.'

'You say that once again, Jock, and I'll . . .'

'OK, OK. What I mean is fuck them.'

'With that?' I asked. 'But I'm inclined to agree.'

And so to a brew-up, beans and bed.

I was about to tuck myself under the tank between the tracks, as had become my habit in clement weather, when Ian came along. He had been prowling round like a maiden aunt with an attack of insomnia.

'Wouldn't do that,' he said. 'Going to rain later; wet ground. Tank will probably sink. Don't want to find you like a pancake under it tomorrow.'

'Strawberry or raspberry,' enquired somebody with a perverted sense of humour.

Ian and I walked for a bit in the darkness. The Germans were sending over a few bits and pieces, not a lot of it, but long-distance heavy stuff.

'It's backs to the wall for them,' said Ian. 'Those shells must be coming straight from the Fatherland itself.'

More locally someone up front was amusing himself playing a tune on a Besa set at single shot: 'Rat. Rat. Rat-tat-tat.' It remineded me of my old squaddie days back in Berwick-upon-Tweed: 'Left, left, left, right, left.'

It was a long night. I think everyone was pretty sure that 'the big one' was fast approaching. It was a bit like boxing. Sitting in your corner with the adrenalin pumping away, waiting for the umpire to call 'seconds out', and bang!—the bell for the final round. Only this fight was to the death.

Dawn broke, the rains came as Ian had predicted, and indeed some of the tanks were in danger of bogging down. It seemed we could never go into battle without an accompaniment of rain, ice or snow. What those poor sods at

Stalingrad must have endured is beyond belief.

As the rain continued to pour down, our infantry started to move up. To my delight they were in support of a brigade of the 51st Highland division. The sight of their dogged cheerfulness raised my spirits as they proceeded to dig in and settle themselves with the phlegmatic efficiency that had served them so well all the way from Tobruk to Long Stop Hill, Sicily, Monte Cassino and onwards. Their battle honours roll off the tongue like a litany.

Briefly I caught sight of an old friend who I had last met leading his company of Argyll and Sutherland Highlanders at the landing.

'You again,' said Joe. 'I'd thought we'd got rid of you away back there.'

He handed me his flask of Army issue rum. 'Better than that bloody Calvados. See you.'

'See you,' I said, as I took a gulp and moved off.

Actually, we were to fight most of the rest of the war together.

That night we had hardly settled down when suddenly the comparative quiet was shattered. The heaviest barrage of the war had started. It seemed as if Monty had ordained that the whole Reichswald should cease to exist. On and on it went. To add to the confusion, occasionally the odd shell would land nearby. It was not clear whether this was the enemy answering back or simply a shortfall of one of our own. To anyone on the receiving end, however, it would not matter much one way or the other.

In the midst of all this mayhem, Monty pulled one of his master strokes. Motorbike dispatch riders came bumping out of the darkness bearing packets of leaflets, plus instructions that all officers down to tank troop or infantry platoon level should personally ensure that every man under their command was made aware of the contents.

This particular exhortation read:

21 ARMY GROUP

PERSONAL MESSAGE

FROM THE C-IN-C

(To be read out to all Troops)

1. The operations of the Allies on all fronts have now brought the German war to its final stage. There was a time, some years ago, when it did not seem possible that we *could* win this war; the present situation is that we cannot lose it: in fact the terrific successes of our Russian allies on the eastern front have brought victory in sight.

2. In 21 Army Group we stand ready for the last round.

   There are many of us who have fought through the previous rounds; we have won every round on points; we now come to the last and final round, and we want, and will go for, the knock-out blow.

3. The rules of the last round will be that we continue fighting till the final count; there is no time limit. We know our enemy well; we must expect him to fight hard to stave off defeat, possibly in the vain hope that we may crack before he does. But we shall not crack; we shall see this thing through to the end.

   The last round may be long and difficult, and the fighting hard; but we now fight on German soil; we have got our opponent where we want him; and he is going to receive the knock-out blow: a somewhat unusual one, delivered from more than one direction.

4. You remember the poem written by a soldier of the Eighth Army in Africa before going into battle, in one verse of which he described what he considered we were fighting for:

   > " Peace for the kids, our brothers freed,
   >   A kinder world, a cleaner breed."

   Let us see to it that we achieve this object, so well expressed by a fighting man of the British Empire.

5. And so we embark on the final round, in close co-operation with our American allies on our right and with complete confidence in the successful outcome of the onslaught being delivered by our Russian allies on the other side of the ring.

   Somewhat curious rules, you may say. But the whole match has been *most* curious; the Germans began this all-out contest and they must not complain when in the last round they are hit from several directions at the same time.

6. Into the ring, then, let us go. And do not let us relax till the knock-out blow has been delivered

7. Good luck to you all—and God bless you.

B. L. Montgomery
Field-Marshal
C-in-C 21 Army Group.

Holland
February, 1945

With the rain coming down ever more torrentially and amid the inferno of noise, bedraggled officers were to be seen struggling from tank to tank, bearing what Monty obviously envisaged as a modern version of the fiery cross. For many of us, this was not his most popular manoeuvre.

Then with dawn about to break, and the barrage if possible becoming more intense, the order came to start up. A few moments later we were trundling up to the start line.

The set-piece attack, timed for a leisurely 1030 hours, went pretty well according to plan. We rumbled forward down the slight incline, our infantry trotting along between the tanks in extended order. My troop was bringing up the rear. The artillery barrage had been directed mainly at the front edge of the forest and it seemed impossible that any enemy had managed to live through it. It was therefore surprising to observe a few of our chaps going down, evidence that some intrepid snipers had hung on.

Before we could reach the trees our tanks were faced with an unexpectedly sticky snag. Nobody had anticipated the heavy rain, or appreciated the fact that there was a marshy ditch about 200 yards short of the edge of the wood. The leading tanks had made heavy weather of it, with the result that by the time our turn came the ditch had been transformed into a rutted morass.

Bill Croaker, my troop sergeant, took a run at it and only just made it. Wally Booth tried to follow him through and stuck. For a moment I had a horrible feeling we were going to be left behind. But who wanted to go into that bloody forest anyway? I suddenly realized that nothing on earth was going to stop me—and the same went for all the rest of us.

I turned my tank round in order to get a longer run at the ditch. Later, Ian told me that he thought I had decided to go home but as the A set was tuned in to Vera Lynn as usual I did not get the benefit of his fairly colourful enquiries.

Choosing some firmer-looking ground, Jock put his foot down and charged like a maddened bull, mud flying in all directions. We must have hit the ditch at about 40 mph, and shuddered almost to a dead halt. Then, miraculously, inch by inch the tank clawed its way on to *terra firma* on the other side.

'Bloody marvellous driving, Jock!' I exclaimed spontaneously.

'I didn't know you cared,' he said calmly. He did not tell me he had nearly knocked himself out with the impact.

To add to Wally's troubles he had thrown a track so it was some three-quarters of an hour later before we got him put together again and hauled him out.

Five minutes later Ian came up on the air: 'Able. Advance. Contact infantry and report.' That was us.

Another ten minutes and I found myself leading the whole British Army along a narrow ride, hemmed in by towering trees and a sitting duck for anyone who might take exception to my

presumption. However, although there were quite a few Germans about, none of them appeared to be carrying anything other than small arms, which was not too surprising. To anticipate tanks motoring about in an almost impenetrable forest would have seemed just about as likely to any thinking man as finding whales in the Round Pond in Kensington Gardens.

In fact as we progressed deeper the trees thinned out somewhat and we had one or two quite good shoots. In places we were even able to get off the restrictions of the rides and flush out the enemy. The result was highly satisfactory and the Seaforths, the leading company, bedded down for the night without casualties.

Fergus, the Seaforth Company Commander, was an extraordinary giant of a man who made me look like a bantam. As if to emphasize his great height, which made him a conspicuous enough target, he strolled around in a full-length white sheepskin coat which must have cost at least half-a-dozen Highland sheep their hides.

It is said that the Scots are a hardy bunch at the best of times, but especially when it comes to the crunch. They are also the first to grab whatever creature comforts are going. When we stopped for the night, Fergus, with a wave of his cromach, had the company batman erect a sizeable mess tent. Long trestle tables and numerous chairs appeared from nowhere and I was formally invited to take drinks with the officers. As dusk fell and the forest filled with sounds of menace, there was a jorum of rum on the table and the sort of convivial conversation one would expect after a successful day's grouse shooting on the moors.

No wonder, I reflected as I staggered back to my tank, that we had won an Empire.

Next morning there was bad news. My lot had slept in the tanks and when we came to shake ourselves out in the morning

I noticed that Jock was looking far from fit. I tried a bit of ribbing but he didn't rise to the occasion. In fact, he seemed to have the utmost difficulty in co-ordinating.

Joe came over and had a look at him. 'Delayed concussion or something. We'd better send him back and let the medics have a look.'

Ian wanted to arrange for a replacement. I didn't much like this idea because I'd rather have moved Geordie into the driver's seat rather than have a new face, even for a short time. Really, my disquiet was a spontaneous expression of how close we had all become in the troop.

Self-congratulation on the success of our advance into the Reichswald the day before proved tragically premature. Lulled into a false sense of security, we were standing around, puffing away at cigarettes and wondering when the order to push on would come through, when there was a sharp report and a young Seaforth lieutenant about ten yards away dropped, blood oozing from his forehead. For a moment everyone froze, but before anyone could run, either to his aid or for cover, another platoon commander crumpled.

It was then that I saw men go wild.

'Come on lads! Get the bastard!' someone shouted. A moment later twenty or thirty men went crashing into the trees. That German sniper must have been a brave—but foolhardy—man. You don't coolly pick off officers in a Highland regiment and expect to get away with it. I never saw the body.

After this incident we ceased to treat the action as a rather pleasant sylvan picnic.

I had moved Geordie into the driver's seat from front gunner and co-driver and we were advancing cautiously ahead of the Jocks. Suddenly a rather breathless, but familiar, apparition appeared alongside. It was Trooper Bolton. It took me a second or two to realize that he was my replacement driver, and I must admit I was rather glad to see him.

'Heard it was you, so I thought I'd take the job,' he volunteered graciously, obviously under the impression that he was doing me a favour. 'Got a fag?' he added inevitably.

It was just like old times.

Day after day the advance through the forest continued. The Seaforths had gone into reserve and had been replaced by the Argyll and Sutherland Highlanders. By a stroke of luck I was to support my friend Joe's company. Joe was a really hard-bitten veteran of the desert days. Several times wounded, he had already won a DSO with bar and a Military Cross. He had a dreadful habit of calling a conference—which I was expected to attend—whenever we ran into a spot of bother. All those invited had to gather round him while he peered at the enemy positions through his binoculars. He would then casually hand them over to someone such as myself for a second opinion. The fact that our rendezvous was usually in full view of the enemy worried him not a jot. He would just lean on his thumb-stick, his silver cap badge—incidentally the largest cap badge of any regiment in the British Army—glinting in the sunshine, and gaze attentively ahead to try and identify the trouble.

At one such conference shells started falling all around us. Everybody, including myself, hit the deck fast, leaving Joe standing alone, leaning on his tall stick. He looked around curiously and remarked:

'What the hell are you all doing down there? They were only our own.'

There was one notable incident in the daily slog which I hesitate to recount, only on the grounds of its improbability. It was getting dark and I was debating whether to pull off the track and settle down for the night. Our routine was that during the hours of daylight we led our infantry, for the reason that behind our armour we were less vulnerable to small-arms fire. At nightfall the infantry would pass through to take up the lead and form a protective screen since they, in turn, were less vulnerable to the armour-piercing bazookas which otherwise could creep up on us under the cover of darkness while we slept.

That particular night, as the dusk was gathering prematurely under the high canopy of trees, I was just about to signal the infantry through when there was the most alarming spurt of flame, followed by a very loud bang indeed. For a moment I thought Joe's tank, which was leading, had been hit by a bazooka shell, but seconds later I heard him come up on the intercom to his driver with such volume that I did not need earphones. There was a crashing of gears, a roaring of engines and Joe charged into the trees. This remarkable escapade was to earn him a doubly-deserved Military Medal.

Where was I, the reader may well ask, while all this banging and crashing was going on? Actually I was in the rear tank with only Wally between me and the action. In fact a second bazooka took a pot-shot at me before Joe blew him up. I can only say that the bazooka operator must have been in a fairly jittery state because at about twenty yards he almost missed completely, the shell passing harmlessly through the back flange of my almost stationary tank.

We were very lucky. An armour-piercing shell amidships is not a pleasant experience. The shell is apt to rattle round the inside of the turret like an angry wasp, causing considerable damage to life and limb before, as likely as not, setting fire to the whole contraption for good measure.

With this excitement over, only the clash of gears could be heard as Joe, Wally and I backed hard into the trees and heaved a sigh of relief as the forward platoon of the Argylls materialized unscathed out of the darkness. A tot or two of the blessed rum and so to bed.

The following morning, as Brigsy reversed the tank back into business, there rose from literally under the left-hand track, with hands held well above his head, as dishevelled, grimy and

altogether miserable a figure as anyone could imagine. His grey German uniform was scarcely recognizable under its coating of mud and oil.

As we stared in amazement at this apparition, he grimaced and pointed to a narrow slit trench in which he had evidently been trapped under the tank track all night. There was something about that gesture which rang the very faintest of bells. I signalled to him to climb on to the turret. Sitting on top of the tank, we just stared at each other in total disbelief.

In those long-ago sunlit days of the 1930s, when God was in his heaven and all was well with the world, my father had decreed that my brother and I should have a German tutor. His name had been Willie Schiller. Now the same Willie Schiller was facing me.

There was nothing much either of us could do about it. He may have said '*Gott in Himmel*,' but I can't really remember. We just had a rum or two and smoked a cigarette. Then I gave Bolton the job of escorting him back to rear HQ.

'See he gets there safely,' I ordered. It was the least I could do. There had been cases, particularly of captured snipers, not making it all the way back.

After the war I was telling my mother about this extraordinary affair.

'Nonsense,' she said firmly. 'It could not have been Willie. You must have been drunk.'

'I was not drunk,' I responded indignantly. 'Why do you say it could not have been Willie?'

'Because,' she said firmly, 'Willie was always so perfectly turned out.'

Three days later we received the order to turn south and emerged from the Reichswald into open country to rejoin the squadron and regroup for the final assault on Goch, which was supposed to open the door for the crossing of the Rhine.

Amazingly, up to that time we had not had a single casualty, apart from Jock's bump on the head.

As we came out of the forest, however, our luck might have changed drastically—at least so far as I personally was concerned. I had stopped the troop just inside the trees and gone forward on foot to where I knew Squadron HQ to be, about 200 yards round the corner. Such was my *joie de vivre* that I broke into a trot down the grass verge alongside the tank-rutted track. Suddenly, looking down, I saw, just where I was about to put my foot, the ominous spikes of an anti-personnel mine. These lethal objects are comparatively small, but anyone unfortunate enough to step on one is immediately made aware of its anti-personnel properties. By some sort of jack-in-the-box spring it jumps into the air and explodes like a fire cracker, scattering ball bearings at just the level calculated to ensure that the victim will have little future as the reproducer of further personnel.

Looking down the grass verge, I could see their little heads about two yards apart, waiting patiently. I slewed off on to the tank track and continued my journey, sweating profusely, at a much more decorous pace.

Happily, the rains had stopped. The ground dried wonderfully and we had two or three glorious days, bivouacked under a hedge with nothing to do but draw our rations and bask in the spring sunshine. Nights were spent squatting in a dry ditch under a tank sheet playing endless games of nap.

Our friends the Argylls were up front, billeted in the little village of Kessel and waiting to move forward, while in the distance a spiralling cloud of smoke, made more dramatic at night by the leaping flames, showed that Goch was well alight. We were now the reserve troop, but it looked as if we might not even be needed on the comparatively short stroll across open ground to the stricken township. However, things seldom turn out as one expects.

It was 2300 hours and we were just thinking about packing in the nap school when Ian came up on the air.

'Move off 0530 hours. Usual friends. Cross start line 0700.'

'What are we supposed to do, give them a piggy-back?' I said. But I was quite glad: my losing streak at nap had seemed endless.

We moved off in darkness, clearing the outskirts of Kessel just as dawn started to break. I was sitting on top of the turret chatting to one or two Jocks who had decided to hitch a ride on the engine covers. Suddenly the tracer started whistling out of the darkness, curving in leisurely arcs like a delivery from a slow off-spin bowler. There was a bit of heavy stuff landing as well. Obviously we were expected.

I pushed forward cautiously with the troop. A mile or so away Goch was blazing merrily but, unbelievably, the strip of narrow ground between the edge of the forest and the road was still held by the Germans in some strength. They were in a suicidal position but obviously had no intention of abandoning it.

As we nosed forward I spotted a stone-built farm building, perhaps a grain store or a cattle shelter. I ordered Bolton to give it a burst or two of tracer. The result exceeded all expectations. There was a moment's pause and then the building lit up like one of the old firework displays at the Crystal Palace. There were vivid flashes, star-spattered explosions and Very lights soaring into the sky, illuminating the whole battlefield as if it were high noon. We had set off a complete ammunition store. The building must have been packed with the stuff.

After about five minutes of pyrotechnics the building blew up in a suitably spectacular finale. Immediately Bunny came up on the intercom. 'Ahead Sir. Look straight ahead.'

I opened the hatches to get a better view and there, as my eyes got accustomed to the natural light, I could see a great column of men moving forward towards us. Through the

174

binoculars I could also see that their arms were slung. A makeshift white flag fluttered and, for good measure, some of the men were waving white handkerchiefs.

I jumped out of my tank and ran over to Joe to find him leaning phlegmatically on his stick.

'They're surrendering!' I shouted, rather wildly. 'It looks like half the bloody German army.'

'I can see that, laddie,' he said in his soft Highland burr. 'Just get back to your wee iron box and see they are not up to any of their tricks.'

As it turned out their surrender was genuine, and, of course, it was not half the German army—just what was left of a proud battalion, defending German soil to the last ditch, literally. As I watched them being marched back over the frontier only two kilometres behind us I felt the joy of battle die in me a little.

By the time we reached Goch it had almost burnt, or been bombed, to the ground, so that it was difficult for the tanks to find a way over the ruined buildings which had collapsed into the streets. As we struggled forward, fearful of casting a track or experiencing some other tiresome and exhausting mishap, there came a sudden deafening roar overhead as three Hurricanes swept low, all guns firing. Nobody seemed to have told them that their job was already completed. As the sound died away the air turned fairly blue, but fortunately there were no casualties.

Making our way back to the squadron laager after what had proved an unexpectedly tiring day, I noticed an acquaintance of mine standing patiently by the roadside. Thinking that somehow he had become unhorsed and in need of a lift I pulled up.

'What's up, Tom?' I asked. 'Want a lift?'

Tom looked at me vaguely as if collecting his thoughts. Then he said with his usual immense civility,

'Awfully kind, old boy, but not to worry. There'll be one along in a minute.'

'One what?'

'An eleven of course. You know what they are. There's not one for simply ages and then about six come all at once.' He gave me a cheery wave of his ash plant. 'Kind of you to stop,' he said.

Suddenly I realized that he was back in the King's Road, Chelsea. His beret had become a bowler hat and his ash plant a neatly rolled umbrella. He was waiting for an eleven bus to take him home to tea after a hard day at the office.

Nothing would move him. All I could do was get on the air and ask for the MO. I did not see Tom again until several years after the war and he had no recollection whatever of the incident. One moment he was leading his troop into battle and the next he was in a comfortable bed in a hospital in Scotland.

Now at last it seemed that there was nothing to stop us crossing the Rhine. The Americans were already over at Remagen in the south. Although we were now fighting on German soil the crossing of the frontier had gone unnoticed. Nobody experienced any sense of historic occasion or could see any reason to hang out flags until we had got to the other side of the river.

In the pause after the Goch incident Joe did organize a celebration, at which I was flattered to be the only outsider invited, but this was really more of a rehearsal for what was planned when we finally made it. Just the same it was a hard night. When the final song had been sung, the final toast drunk and the final pledge of eternal friendship plighted, I stumbled out into the cool dawn to watch the sun rise over Westphalia.

'Ich weiss nicht was soll es bedeuten,
Dass ich so traurig bin . . .

The haunting words of Heinrich Heine's 'Die Lorelei' came unbidden. Had it been Willie Schiller who had first taught me to appreciate the beauty of the German language, so often regarded as guttural and ugly? Only ten kilometres further on the Rhine flowed quietly. The flood which was about to overwhelm the '*Schiffer und Kahn*' of Nazi Germany was building up against the dam. Was Heine, the Jew, laughing on his cloud above Parnassus? I think not.

CHAPTER 14

We were all sitting round in the comfortable room which served as the officers' mess in the farmhouse we had requisitioned. It was our first time together as a squadron and actually under a roof. From before the battle of the Reichswald I had scarcely seen my fellow troop leaders. We had a lot to talk about—and laugh about—a lot of leg pulling and a lot of just enjoying each other's company.

The more strategically minded among us were concerned with just when and how we would be involved in the final crossing of the Rhine. Someone introduced a strong rumour that a brand-new tank weapon had been devised which, instead of a gun, had a turret fitted with a blinding light. He said that this was to be used as our secret weapon to light our way over the river, to the great discomfiture of the enemy.

I listened in amazement. Could it possibly be that someone had at last literally 'seen the light' and that, after all, my old friend the Canal Defence Light was to have a part to play in the final victory? I looked forward to finding out with mixed feelings.

On the fourth day Ian strolled into the mess.

'I have a message for you,' he said. 'It's your hairy haggis-bashers. They need you.'

'You can take a joke too far,' I retorted.

'They seem to have run up against another pocket of resistance.'

'They have a certain knack of doing just that.'

He handed me a piece of paper. 'That's the map reference. Be there 1700 hours. Oh, and by the way, it's to be a night attack.'

Very soon we were all once again lined up behind a hedge, in the pouring rain as usual, waiting for night to fall. At least it made a change from waiting for dawn to break.

The view through my binoculars was bleak—a rutted track running across fields as flat as Salisbury Plain and twice as soggy. Odd farmhouses were dotted here and there in the distance.

Then a few desultory shells started coming over from where the pocket of resistance was supposed to be, plopping despondently into the mud. One landed by the track and immediately set off two other rather bigger explosions. I made a mental correction to my previous observation: flat as Salisbury Plain, twice as soggy—and mined.

The first wave of the Argylls disappeared into the darkness. We started up and trundled along, keeping the second wave company and well clear of the track. We'd advanced about 800 yards when it all began to happen. The sky was suddenly illuminated by half a dozen enemy Very lights, followed by the familiar crackle of spandau fire. The first wave hit the ground sharpish, except of course for Joe, who I could see momentarily silhouetted against the skyline, waving his thumb-stick and no doubt making some colourful comments on the situation.

It was our turn to take over. As we speeded up it was a mystery to me where the opposition was hiding itself. So far as I could see, the fire was coming from the middle of flat ground with not enough cover to hide a fieldmouse. We were advancing in V-formation, with my tank a good hundred yards or so ahead of the other two, when, as another flare went up, all was revealed. Right across the front the enemy had dug an enormous ditch from which point of concealment they were pumping everything they had got at our side.

It was not only a good defensive position but it also provided, from the German point of view, the ideal tank trap. And we were heading for it at full gallop.

I grabbed the microphone to give the order for our lot to halt until I could re-evaluate the situation. At that precise moment the wireless set elected to go dead. Out in the darkness I could hear Bill and Wally grinding remorselessly forward. Unless another flare went up they would not see the danger until it was too late.

'For Chrissake someone stop the buggers!' I yelled, but there was little hope that there was anyone to hear. Suddenly the front hatch burst open and Bolton splashed off into the darkness, yelling fit to wake the dead and with the spandau bullets buzzing like fireflies round his ears.

God alone knows how, but he managed to halt my two stable-mates. Then he was clambering back on to the tank and I realized for the first time where the expression 'swearing like a trooper' came from.

'You all right?' I asked.

'No, I'm not bleedin' fuckin'-well all right!'

'Did you get hit?'

'Course I got bloody hit!'

'Well, don't hang around. Get in and put that hatch down.'

'Can't.'

'Why not?'

'Well, I got it in the arse, didn't I? How can I ruddy-well sit in there with a bleedin' bullet in me arse?'

At this latest disaster in Bolton's military career, I am afraid we all fell apart laughing—but it made him none the less of a 'bleedin' 'ero'.

By this time the Germans had stopped letting off flares and slackened off the spandau fire. I thus deduced that they were preparing to withdraw to their next line of defence, wherever that might be, under cover of darkness. We started letting off random bursts of tracer bullets to try and see what was going on and once again fortune was on our side.

Some tracer hit a haybarn about 800 yards beyond the ditch and within seconds it became a blazing torch, illuminating the whole countryside—only this time it was the German positions that were illuminated and we who were in darkness.

At this turn of events our Highland friends decided that they had had enough of the indignity of crouching in water-filled shell-holes and they set off in hot pursuit of the retreating enemy, uttering wild Gaelic cries as an aid to circulation. With some difficulty I found a way round the ditch and set off in an effort to catch up with them.

Suddenly there was a red flash, an extra loud bang, and I distinctly heard Wally, who was right behind me, exclaim over the B set! 'Bloody hell. Duggie's bought it.'

Since these are not posthumous memoirs, he was obviously mistaken. I'd just had an anti-tank mine blow off my left track. We all got out and walked back to Wally's tank. After half an hour of hanging about wondering whether anybody wanted us any more, Ian came on the air.

'Come back,' he said. 'All is forgiven.' Or words to that effect.

Well, that was more or less the end of Sutherland's war. Back at squadron HQ I apologized to Ian for the state of Bolton's arse and for having to abandon my tank. His reaction was to dole out rather more than my unexpended ration of rum, with the odd whisky from his personal bottle thrown in for good measure. Then he told me the latest news.

The small matter of the crossing of the Rhine in the British sector was considered all over bar the shouting. We knew that the Americans had made it across at Remagen in the south. Thus the Hun was well and truly on the run.

For us, all that was expected was to counter any token resistance by what amounted to a few *Hitler Jugend*. Apart from that, our brigade was going into mothballs in a German hutted camp while the Guards and the gallant 51st Highland Division made the actual crossing. The Royal Engineers were already standing by to throw a Bailey bridge or two across, on which we tankies would be able to cross in comfort when our turn came.

Strange as it may seem, most of us were highly frustrated by our lack of participation in the coming events. Although we were thoroughly exhausted, it still would have proved highly satisfactory to have seen the ball over the line rather than leaving the glory to someone else.

Still, there were compensations. The German barracks proved relatively comfortable, waterproof and undamaged, which was more than one could say about most of the surrounding countryside.

One morning we were aroused by the drone of heavy aircraft and, rushing outside, watched in awe as a glider-towing armada of planes flew low over our heads. We waved and cheered but I doubt if anyone up there took much notice. They were only five minutes away from their moment of truth.

Later we heard that the crossing had not been such a doddle after all. Major-General Neil Ritchie, one of the greatest soldiers ever to command the 51st Highland Division, had been killed by an unlucky mortar shell which landed in his DUKW half-way across the river. Up front my mate Joe of the 7th Argylls had pushed his luck once too often. He survived, but lost both his legs.

Bolton reappeared one day, walking a little stiffly but announcing that he was now quite ready to be driven on the last stage of the journey.

Somehow sacks of mail began to get through. I and some others got a letter from Lady Bonham-Carter wondering whether we would care to vote Liberal at the next election.

Everyone received a letter from Lord Vansittart, instructing us not to go soft on the Germans at the moment of victory but to go on hating them for ever and ever.

Our turn to cross the Rhine came as rather an anticlimax but it did at least give us the feeling that we were at last on German soil. We tooled rather aimlessly across the Westphalian plains. Occasionally, rumbling through a village, somebody would take a pot-shot at us, or more usually some little ragamuffin would dart out of an alley, hurl a stone and beat a hasty retreat.

Further ahead there was some spasmodic resistance and sometimes we heard the sound of distant gunfire. Of the Germans whom we passed by on the roadside, one could only sense their dispiritedness and resignation. There must have been few of the elderly, staring at us with lacklustre eyes, who had not lost somebody dear. It was an immensely depressing experience.

Just occasionally someone would raise a hand half-heartedly, whether in greeting or in admission of defeat it was hard to tell. The impulse to wave back was almost irresistible but it was against the rules. 'No fraternization' was the order and that meant that it was breaking regulations even to bid someone a civil 'good morning'.

That night I got out Lord Vansittart's mandamus and read it over again. I sat for a moment. Then I lit a match, held it to the paper, and watched it as it burned.